COMPACT

ADVANCED

SECOND EDITION

C1

WORKBOOK
WITH DIGITAL PACK

Helen Tiliouine

Shaftesbury Road, Cambridge CB2 8EA, United Kingdom

One Liberty Plaza, 20th Floor, New York, NY 10006, USA

477 Williamstown Road, Port Melbourne, VIC 3207, Australia

314–321, 3rd Floor, Plot 3, Splendor Forum, Jasola District Centre, New Delhi – 110025, India

103 Penang Road, #05–06/07, Visioncrest Commercial, Singapore 238467

Cambridge University Press & Assessment is a department of the University of Cambridge.

We share the University's mission to contribute to society through the pursuit of education, learning and research at the highest international levels of excellence.

www.cambridge.org
Information on this title: www.cambridge.org/9781009394925

© Cambridge University Press & Assessment 2014, 2024

This publication is in copyright. Subject to statutory exception and to the provisions of relevant collective licensing agreements, no reproduction of any part may take place without the written permission of Cambridge University Press & Assessment.

First published 2014
Second edition 2024
20 19 18 17 16 15 14 13 12 11 10 9 8 7 6 5 4 3 2 1

Printed in Dubai by Oriental Press

A catalogue record for this publication is available from the British Library

ISBN 978-1-009-39492-5 Workbook

Additional resources for this publication at www.cambridge.org/compact

Cambridge University Press & Assessment has no responsibility for the persistence or accuracy of URLs for external or third-party internet websites referred to in this publication and does not guarantee that any content on such websites is, or will remain, accurate or appropriate.

Contents

1	Communication and language	6
2	Travel and culture	10
3	Getting along	14
4	Making ends meet	18
5	Well-being and sport	22
6	Art and entertainment	26
7	Green living	30
8	Learn and earn	34
9	Technically speaking	38
10	All in the mind	42

C1 Advanced Exam information	46
Acknowledgements	47

Material available online:

Answer key and audio scripts

MAP OF THE UNITS

UNIT	TOPICS	GRAMMAR	VOCABULARY
1 Communication and language	Communication and language	Review of verb tenses	Collocations
2 Travel and culture	Travel, culture and traditions	Participle clauses	Prefixes
3 Getting along	Human behaviour and relationships	Reported speech	Idioms with *keep*
4 Making ends meet	Money and business	Passive and causative verb forms	Money vocabulary
5 Well-being and sport	Well-being and sport	Conditional forms	Word building Suffixes
6 Art and entertainment	The arts and entertainment	Verbs followed by the infinitive and/or *-ing*	Frequently confused words
7 Green living	Nature and the environment	Inversion of subject and verb	Environment vocabulary Idioms: nature
8 Learn and earn	Education, learning and work	Relative clauses	Spelling changes
9 Technically speaking	Science and technology	Modal verbs	Science vocabulary
10 All in the mind	Psychology and personality	Wishes and regrets	Three-part phrasal verbs Adjectives of personality

READING	USE OF ENGLISH	WRITING	LISTENING
Part 7: gapped text	Part 1: multiple-choice cloze	Part 1 essay: getting ideas, contrast links, checking	Part 4: multiple matching
Part 6: cross-text multiple matching	Part 3: word formation	Part 2 report: planning, recommending	Part 2: sentence completion
Part 5: multiple-choice questions	Part 4: key word transformations	Part 2 email: register	Part 1: short texts, multiple-choice questions
Part 7: gapped text	Part 2: open cloze	Part 1 essay: addition links, achieving balance	Part 3: long text, multiple-choice questions
Part 8: multiple matching	Part 3: word formation	Part 2 proposal: purpose links, text organisation	Part 2: sentence completion
Part 5: multiple-choice questions	Part 1: multiple-choice cloze	Part 2 review: praising and criticising	Part 4: multiple matching
Part 7: gapped text	Part 4: key word transformations	Part 1 essay: sentence adverbs, paraphrasing notes	Part 1: short texts, multiple-choice questions
Part 8: multiple matching	Part 3: word formation	Part 2 formal letter: formal language	Part 2: sentence completion
Part 5: multiple-choice questions	Part 2: open cloze	Part 2 report: result links, text organisation	Part 3: long text, multiple-choice questions
Part 6: cross-text multiple matching	Part 4: key word transformations	Part 1 essay: concession	Part 4: multiple matching

MAP OF THE UNITS 5

1 Communication and language

Reading and Use of English
Part 7

1 Look at the exam task and read the article quickly, ignoring the gaps. Then answer these questions.

1 What does the word *dialect* mean?
2 How do many people feel about dialects?
3 What has research shown about speaking two dialects?

✓ **Exam task**

2 You are going to read an article about research into language speaking. Six paragraphs have been removed from the extract. Choose from the paragraphs **A–G** the one which fits each gap (**1–6**). There is one extra paragraph which you do not need to use.

The value of speaking dialects

A researcher explains how speaking different dialects may be as beneficial as speaking different languages.

There has been a lot of research to back up the idea that people who use two or more languages every day experience significant advantages. The brain-training involved in having to use a different language depending on the context and speaker is credited with enhancing attention and memory skills. But there is another source of brain-training connected with language use: dialects – different forms of the same language which are spoken in particular parts of a country. Bi-dialectalism, which simply means the regular use of two different dialects, is widespread globally. In the US, for example, millions of children grow up speaking African American Vernacular English at home, as well as mainstream American English at school.

1

This reflects the way in which people who use two varieties of the same language often consider the regional variation they speak to be of lesser value than the official version of their language. However, it is a mistake to think of dialects as somehow inferior to official languages.

2

Moreover, what our research suggests is that people who speak two dialects may share a number of mental abilities with people who speak two languages. For the human mind, it seems that speaking two dialects may be as useful when it comes to developing thinking skills as speaking two completely different languages.

3

Our study included 64 of these bi-dialectal children, 47 multilingual children and 25 children who only spoke one language. Comparisons between the three groups were carried out in two stages, and the socio-economic status, language proficiency and general intelligence of all children taking part were taken into account.

4

Somewhat to our surprise, the multilingual and bi-dialectal children did better in the tests than those who only spoke one language. Another recent study investigated the educational achievement of some Norwegian children who are taught to write in two forms, reflecting two different Norwegian dialects. In standardised national tests, the children who were taught to write in both dialectal forms had scores higher than the national average.

5

They could be dialects of the same language, two related languages such as Italian and Spanish, or languages as diverse as English and Mandarin Chinese. Systematically switching between any two forms of language, even quite similar ones, appears to stimulate the mind and lead to higher cognitive performance. It therefore looks as if – contrary to some widely held beliefs – when it comes to language, any degree of diversity is an advantage. In this respect, dialects are clearly under-recognised and undervalued.

6

For instance, we are now investigating its impact on understanding implied meaning in conversation – in other words, whether the experience of anticipating which language a speaker will use makes bilingual and bi-dialectal children better able to read the speaker's intentions more generally – and more specifically, understanding the real meaning of what they say. It is a fascinating field to be working in and there is certainly plenty more to find out!

UNIT 1 COMMUNICATION AND LANGUAGE

A In fact, what we call 'the language' of a country, such as Italian, is simply one of a number of linguistically related varieties that, for cultural, historical and political reasons, was chosen as the standard variety.

B The situation may well improve in future, but it is worth emphasising that so far, much of the research on bilingualism has focused on a relatively narrow range of thinking skills. However, new studies are looking into the broader effects of speaking more than one language or dialect.

C Participants had to recall digits in the reverse order of presentation. That is, if presented with 'three, nine, five, six', they had to recall 'six, five, nine, three'. This allowed us to measure their ability to recall and manipulate information.

D As a result, when children are at school, the influence of dialects is far greater than most people realise. Our research may help to evaluate their impact and why attitudes to them are changing in many parts of the world.

E Similar situations arise in the Arab-speaking world, as well as in many parts of Europe, such as the German-speaking parts of Switzerland. Children there may only feel comfortable talking in High German when in class, but switch to Swiss-German for everyday conversation.

F Both these studies suggest that advantages previously reported for multilingual children could be shared by children speaking two or more dialects. It seems the advantages of bilingualism arise with any combination of language varieties that differ enough to challenge the brain.

G We tested the mental performance of children, including some who grew up speaking both Cypriot Greek and Standard Modern Greek. These are two varieties of Greek which are closely related but differ from each other on all levels of language analysis (vocabulary, pronunciation and grammar).

Part 1

3 Look at the exam task. Quickly read the text without filling the gaps and answer these questions.

1 When were emojis invented?
2 How can they help with science communication?
3 What were emojis first used for?

✓ Exam task

4 For questions **1–8**, read the text below and decide which answer (**A**, **B**, **C** or **D**) best fits each gap. There is an example at the beginning (**0**).

Example:
0 A heads   B stems   C flows   D issues

Using emojis in science communication

Emojis are 'picture characters' whose name (0) ....B.... from the Japanese 'e' (picture) and 'moji' (character). Since the first emoji was created in the late 1990s, they have become popular as a form of visual communication (1) .... specific emotional responses. They can be an easily accessible visual language, and in the world of science communication, they may help to (2) .... digital audiences and maintain an informal tone.

Nevertheless, although emojis were initially developed to (3) .... email and professional communication, using them may be regarded as (4) .... in fields such as science, journalism and law. Including emojis in online science dialogue therefore involves a (5) .... balancing act: enhancing scientific communication with these visual (6) ...., but making sure never to rely (7) .... on them to convey meaning.

Science communicators also need to thoroughly understand their target audiences in order to ensure
that specific emojis are interpreted as intended. Unless readers understand why emojis are being used, these can become a form of visual (8) ...., and therefore be misinterpreted or exclude some readers.

1 A directing   B pointing   C referring   D indicating
2 A associate   B engage   C feature   D appeal
3 A feed   B raise   C aid   D please
4 A inappropriate B unqualified   C disadvantaged   D imperfect
5 A narrow   B graceful   C delicate   D gentle
6 A appliances   B tools   C agents   D gadgets
7 A solely   B alone   C extremely   D overall
8 A speech   B tongue   C vocabulary   D jargon

UNIT 1 COMMUNICATION AND LANGUAGE   7

Listening

Part 4

1 Look at the exam task instructions and answer these questions.

1 What will each extract be about?
2 How many questions do you have to answer for each speaker?
3 Can you choose the same letter for two different speakers in one task?

✓ **Exam task**

 2 🔊 02 You will hear five short extracts in which people are talking about misunderstandings.

While you listen, you must complete both tasks.

TASK ONE

For questions **1–5**, choose from the list (**A–H**) how each speaker felt about the misunderstanding.

A annoyed by how time-consuming it was
B pleased to have avoided sounding aggressive
C amazed by how persuasive the other person was
D determined to avoid repeating their mistake
E convinced the other person was joking
F relieved the other person was talkative
G shocked at how upsetting it was
H concerned about causing trouble

Speaker 1	1
Speaker 2	2
Speaker 3	3
Speaker 4	4
Speaker 5	5

TASK TWO

For questions **6–10**, choose from the list (**A–H**) how each speaker resolved the problem.

A They apologised immediately.
B They promised to return a favour.
C They updated some information.
D They changed their plans.
E They provided some evidence.
F They admitted to being easily distracted.
G They sent someone a present.
H They arranged an online meeting.

Speaker 1	6
Speaker 2	7
Speaker 3	8
Speaker 4	9
Speaker 5	10

Grammar

Review of verb tenses

1 Choose the correct form of the verb in each sentence.

1 By the time we got round to booking tickets for the concert, the only seats left **were** / **had been** / **will have been** unaffordable.
2 I can't give a definite answer until **I'm going to have** / **I'll have** / **I have** more information.
3 When I got to the café, my friend **was** / **had been** / **has been** there for half an hour and was looking rather grumpy.
4 I hope **I'll find out** / **I'm finding out** / **I'd found out** if I've got the job before the end of the month!
5 By this time next week, **I'm moving** / **I'll have moved** / **I'll have been moving** into my new flat!
6 I'll drop a hint to my aunt and uncle about what I want for my birthday when **I'll see** / **I see** / **I'm seeing** them next week.
7 Mark **has been working** / **was working** / **is working** in this office since he finished college.
8 I want you all to know that Julia **would play** / **will have played** / **will be playing** an important role in the business from now on.

2 Complete the sentences with the correct form of a verb in the box.

| become | meet | reach | talk | try |

1 Do you think you'll feel self-conscious when you .... your new colleagues?
2 I .... to learn French for many years now, but I'm not sure I'll ever be able to make myself understood!
3 I think they .... business when I arrived, but I can't be sure, because the restaurant was very noisy.
4 At exactly this time tomorrow, we .... the end of our journey!
5 This technology .... completely obsolete by the end of this century.

3 🎯 Tick the correct sentences written by exam candidates. Correct the sentences with mistakes.

1 We will pay for the work you had done for us so far.
2 When I'm free, I'll go on the computer and get some more information.
3 Internet use is booming recently amongst older people.
4 By the end of the journey, you will have been driving for hours and hours.
5 The holiday activities are very different from what we used to doing in our everyday lives.

UNIT 1 COMMUNICATION AND LANGUAGE

Writing

Part 1 essay

Contrast links

1 Choose a word or expression from the box to complete each sentence.

> Contrary   Despite   In contrast   Whereas

1 .... the fact that I can make myself understood in several foreign languages, I can't hold long conversations in any of them.

2 .... to what many people think, posting comments is often an insecure form of communication.

3 .... my sister's very outgoing and imaginative, my brother's quite self-centred.

4 My grandmother only used her phone very rarely. ...., I carry mine with me everywhere.

2 Look at this exam task and answer these questions.

1 Do you need to discuss all three ways of communicating with friends?

2 How many of the opinions from the discussion should you use?

☑ Exam task

Your class has just had a discussion on how people communicate and how they maintain long-term friendships and relationships with others. You have made the notes below.

> **Ways of communicating**
> - being in the same room, chatting face-to-face
> - talking together on video calls
> - sending text messages
>
> Some opinions expressed in the discussion:
> 'I like being able to see people's body language.'
> 'It's good to be able to talk to people all over the world.'
> 'You can reply whenever you feel like it.'

Write an essay discussing **two** of the ways of communicating in your notes. You should **explain which way you think is better for maintaining long-term relationships with other people, giving reasons** to support your opinion.

You may, if you wish, make use of the opinions expressed in the discussion, but you should use your own words as far as possible.

3 Choose the correct contrast links to complete the essay below.

These days, it is remarkably easy to communicate with people all over the world. This means that we should all find it easier to maintain long-term relationships, too. **(1) Conversely / Nevertheless / Even though,** that is not always the case, unfortunately.

(2) While / In spite of / However people can send messages to one another at any time of day or night, and reply to them at their convenience, there is always the potential for misunderstandings. It is also easy to forget to respond, sometimes for days and weeks on end. **(3) Whereas / Although / However,** it can also keep relationships alive which might otherwise fade away through lack of any kind of contact.

Actually being in the same place, communicating directly face-to-face, may seem to be the best way to ensure true understanding between people. After all, a few words on a screen can never beat actually seeing someone's reaction to what is being said. **(4) On the other hand / While / Despite the fact,** with the busy lives that people increasingly lead, this can be more and more of a challenge to arrange, especially for people living in different parts of the world. When the choice is between imperfect communication and losing touch completely, many people will opt for the former.

On balance, in my personal opinion, **(5) conversely / despite / although** its limitations, text messaging can often be a better means of staying in touch with others over the years than meeting in person. Insisting on meeting in person can simply be impractical, and surely some kind of contact with those we care for is better than none at all.

☑ Exam task

4 Your class has had a discussion on whether people need to learn different languages. You have made the notes below.

> **Why people learn different languages**
> - to improve their work prospects
> - to make friends from various countries
> - to explore other cultures
>
> Some opinions expressed in the discussion:
> 'The most interesting jobs involve speaking several languages.'
> 'To really understand someone, you need to speak their language.'
> 'Books that have been translated aren't worth reading.'

Write an essay for your tutor discussing two of the ideas in your notes. You should **explain which is the most likely motivation for people to learn another language, giving reasons** to support your opinion.

You may, if you wish, make use of the opinions expressed in the discussion, but you should use your own words as far as possible.

Write your **essay** in **220–260** words in an appropriate style.

UNIT 1 COMMUNICATION AND LANGUAGE   9

2 Travel and culture

Reading and Use of English

Part 6

1 Look at the exam task and answer these questions.

1 Are the four texts on the same topic?
2 Do the writers of the texts all have similar opinions?

✓ Exam task

2 You are going to read four extracts from articles in which experts give their views on ecotourism. For questions **1–4**, choose from the writers **A–D**. The writers may be chosen more than once.

Which writer

1 shares a view with B on whether ecotourism brings benefits to local people? **1** ☐

2 has a different opinion from C regarding ecotourism's contribution to countries' economic development? **2** ☐

3 has a similar opinion to D on the extent to which ecotourism helps to preserve the local environment? **3** ☐

4 expresses a different view from all the others on whether ecotourism has an impact on visitors' daily lives once they have returned home? **4** ☐

A

Ecotourism is a form of tourism involving travel by sustainable means to natural areas, and aims both to conserve the environment and improve the well-being of the people who live there. However, does the reality of ecotourism live up to these admirable goals? Undoubtedly, in some respects; the money raised from such trips can be used to protect endangered species and their habitats, which might otherwise disappear from the face of our planet. As for the people, though, not enough is always done to prevent them becoming tourist attractions themselves, somehow part of the package on offer. At a national level, ecotourism clearly brings in much needed revenue, and can encourage tourists to visit other areas, too. And what of the ecotourists themselves? Many report having their eyes opened to aspects of environmentalism that they had never considered previously, and say that this has changed their habits and world view for ever.

B

Although ecotours were relatively rare only a few years ago, there are now many possible destinations for anyone interested in joining one. The experience is evidently one that will never be forgotten, and frequently results in long-term alterations to individuals' lifestyles. And for those who were born in these remote places, ecotourism means they are now able to find decently paid jobs in their area that never existed previously. This allows them to stay where they want to be rather than find themselves forced to move away to improve their work prospects. Ecotourism, it would seem, is a win-win situation for all concerned. And yet, despite people's best intentions, harm occurs: vegetation is damaged by visitors on hikes, some rubbish is inevitably left behind. As the popularity of ecotourism steadily grows, care must be taken for it not to end up creating more problems than it solves.

C

Ecotourism has become more and more common recently, with ecotourists visiting parts of their own country or travelling abroad. However, those trying to persuade governments of the advantages of ecotourism need to bear in mind that the income generated is fairly insignificant compared with the wealth created by mass tourism. Nevertheless, there is, fortunately, increasing acceptance of the need to promote the protection and conservation of nature, and ecotourism certainly supports this worthy ambition. The tourists themselves, of course, are usually already very well informed about the need to conserve Earth's fragile ecosystems, so I would say that taking part in an ecotour is unlikely to modify their behaviour in any fundamental way. On the other hand, such tours are a valuable opportunity for cultural exchange between tourists and residents. Greater awareness of – and respect for – the customs and traditions of the people visited can surely only be a positive outcome.

D

Ecotourism is sometimes claimed to be a major part of the solution for natural areas under threat. Personally, I cannot see how encouraging ever larger numbers of visitors to these places can be said to be beneficial. After all, strangers risk introducing plant and animal diseases, thus potentially achieving the very opposite of what ecotourism is intended to bring about. I must admit, though, that it will probably affect the way participants in these tours look at the world, encouraging them to make greater efforts to preserve the nature nearer their own homes. Those native to many ecotour destinations, however, can feel they lack control over the speed and degree of development in their region brought about by this type of tourism. In this respect, it can be as problematic as more traditional forms of tourism. Moreover, ecotours are often relatively cheap, with people spending comparatively little in the country they are visiting.

Grammar
Participle clauses

1 Rewrite these sentences using participle clauses.

1 The woman who is sitting over there is a famous climber.
....
2 I didn't take a waterproof jacket, so I got completely soaked.
....
3 As Selma walked along a path by the river, she watched some swans land on the water.
....
4 She missed her bus three times last week, so she's now getting up half an hour earlier.
....
5 As long as you approach the monkeys slowly, they won't bite.
....
6 After I successfully took part in a ten-kilometre race, I started training for a marathon.
....

2 There is one correct and one incorrect sentence in each of the following pairs. Tick the correct sentences.

1 A Having heard how it ended, the film wasn't very exciting for me.
  B Having heard how it ended, I didn't find the film very exciting.
2 A We had a great trip organised by a reputable travel company.
  B Organised by a reputable travel company, we had a great trip.
3 A Rehearsing for a concert, they had a picnic in the park and listened to some musicians.
  B They had a picnic in the park and listened to some musicians rehearsing for a concert.
4 A Not having seen her for ages, Maria looked completely different.
  B Not having seen her for ages, I didn't recognise Maria at first.
5 A Unopened, you can keep this strawberry jam for a year.
  B Unopened, this strawberry jam can be kept for a year.

3 Join the sentences using participle clauses.

1 Laurie sat aboard the train. She realised she had left a bag on the platform.
....
2 Gerda walked away from the village. She didn't look back.
Without ....
3 I hoped to get a good photograph of the lake at dawn. I set off before sunrise.
....
4 We couldn't speak the local language. We couldn't follow the story.
....
5 They planned their itinerary carefully. They didn't waste any time.
....

Reading and Use of English
Part 3
Vocabulary – Prefixes

1 Add the correct prefixes to complete the words in bold.

1 In this part of the city, some of the ....**habitants** are very affluent.
2 Do you think it's ....**realistic** to expect all public transport to be free?
3 The water level in the lake has ....**creased** over the past few years because of the lack of rain.
4 The instructions were ....**precise**, so I got confused.
5 When I was a child, subsidies for rail travel were ....**existent**.
6 People have expressed their ....**satisfaction** with the level of emissions in the town.
7 The downside of that surf school is that most of the instructors are ....**experienced**.
8 The people in that carriage were very ....**polite**, so I moved to a different part of the train.

2 Choose the correct words in these sentences.

1 The **reaction** / **interaction** between the actors was very convincing.
2 My mother is French and my father is Chinese, so I'm **bilingual** / **monolingual**.
3 The musician says he's **underpaid** / **overpaid**, so he's looking for another job.
4 Many people are opposed to the proposed **redevelopment** / **underdevelopment** of the city centre.
5 Boys **renumber** / **outnumber** girls in my acting class, but that isn't the norm at my school.

UNIT 2 TRAVEL AND CULTURE

3 Look at the exam task instructions and quickly read the text. What examples does the writer give of difficulties that travellers may experience?

✓ **Exam task**

4 For questions **1–8**, read the text below. Use the word given in capitals at the end of some of the lines to form a word that fits in the gap **in the same line**. There is an example at the beginning (**0**).

Write your answers **IN CAPITAL LETTERS**.

Example: (0) STRIKING

Travel can make you smarter!

According to research, one of the most (**0**) .... effects of travel on the human mind is how it encourages us to be more creative. It seems that experiencing a (**1**) .... of customs and traditions is good for the brain, as it is being forced to find probable (**2**) .... for people's behaviour in circumstances that are unfamiliar to us. (**3**) ...., when travellers experience confusion, such as wondering whether to tip in a café, or where a train is actually taking them, their minds are developing.	**STRIKE** **DIVERSE** **EXPLAIN** **BASE**
Travel is not always easy, and problems are often (**4**) .... However, if travellers were aware of the fact that all the (**5**) .... they have to tolerate are in fact boosting their thinking skills, they might find them easier to bear.	**AVOID** **COMFORT**
An (**6**) .... to understand what people are saying and doing may not be as bad as it appears at the time. The (**7**) .... to and observation of cultural contrasts brings long-term benefits, it seems, because these differences are what stimulate our (**8**)	**ABLE** **EXPOSE** **CREATE**

Listening

Part 2

✓ **Exam task**

1 🔊 **03** You will hear a man called Murat Kaya talking to a group of students about a canoe trip along the River Severn, in the UK. For questions **1–8**, complete the sentences with a word or short phrase.

CANOE TRIP
ALONG THE RIVER SEVERN

Murat chose to stay overnight in
(**1**) .... during his trip.
Murat's luggage was transported in a
(**2**) .... throughout the trip.
Murat says the term 'sweepers' is used for tree
(**3**) .... that can cause problems for canoeists.
The only birds that Murat was a little nervous about were the (**4**) .... he often saw.
Murat says that having (**5**) .... was the most uncomfortable thing about being in the canoe.
Some of the towns along Murat's route are frequently affected by (**6**) .... nowadays.
Murat canoed under a famous bridge made of
(**7**) ....
Murat uses the word (**8**) '..................' to describe his canoe trip.

UNIT 2 TRAVEL AND CULTURE

Writing

Part 2 report

1 Which of the following sentences are correct? Correct the mistakes in the other sentences.

1 On a balance, people are in favour of this idea.
2 Some charities should be established with the aim of helping the homeless.
3 To summing up, a new sports centre would benefit the local residents.
4 This report aims to evaluate the success of the new education policy.
5 Adopting these suggestions, I believe we would raise the level of job satisfaction among staff.
6 Basing on all the points mentioned above, we recommend the following improvements.
7 I'd like to suggest some changes to the timetable.
8 Shortly, this is the most cost-effective solution.

2 Read the exam task below and answer these questions.

1 How many places must you write about?
2 What do *it* and *there* refer to in bullet points 2 and 3?
3 Who might be interested in reading your suggestions in response to the third bullet point?

✓ Exam task

Your college class recently went on an educational trip to a town or city. Now your English teacher has asked you to write a report on the trip.

In your report you should:
- briefly describe the town or city visited
- explain how enjoyable it was to visit
- suggest ways in which future college trips there could be improved.

Write your **report** in **220–260** words in an appropriate style.

3 Quickly read the model report, *Visiting Oxford*, and match the content a–e with each paragraph.

a good things about visiting Oxford
b some possible ways to improve future trips
c what the report will be about
d what was not so good about visiting Oxford
e some basic information about the city of Oxford

Visiting Oxford

Introduction

1 The (1) .... of this report is to describe the recent trip to Oxford organised for students from our college. The report will (2) .... both positive and negative aspects of the visit, and suggest some possible (3) .... to the problems encountered.

The City of Oxford

2 Oxford is a small city, home to a world-famous university and many beautiful historical buildings. There are numerous places to visit, (4) .... the university colleges, several museums and many green spaces.

Enjoyable features of the visit

3 The students found the university colleges fascinating. Because most of these are in the centre, they were easy to reach on foot. There was a wide choice of restaurants and cafés for lunch, and many students said that their trip on the river afterwards, in boats called 'punts', was hilarious.

What could be improved

4 In the morning, the students visited the city centre independently, before gathering after lunch for the river trip. However, the colleges are not all open at the same time, and while some charge small entrance fees, others do not. (5) ...., the maps displayed in the city centre are not all up-to-date, and there are few signs directing people towards the sights. In (6) ...., some students felt they did not see as much as they might have done.

(7) ....

5 It would be worth (8) .... making students aware of the local visitor apps. They (9) .... be given clear information about college opening times and charges. Another (10) .... of action might be to arrange for the students to be given a guided tour in the morning instead of exploring the city on their own.

4 Complete each gap in the report with a word from the box.

considering   course   including   moreover
outline   purpose   recommendations
short   should   solutions

5 Write your own report in answer to the same exam task. Write 220–260 words in an appropriate style.

UNIT 2 TRAVEL AND CULTURE 13

3 Getting along

Reading and Use of English
Part 5

✓ **Exam task**

1 You are going to read an article about friendship. For questions **1–6**, choose the answer (**A**, **B**, **C** or **D**) which you think fits best according to the text.

Friendship

Cathy Mason considers what the novelist and philosopher Iris Murdoch can teach us about friendship.

Making friends might come easier to some people than others, but in general, we all use the same criteria for forming relationships. We are drawn to people who share our interests, or whom we simply like and admire. Once we make friends, we tend to have a very good opinion of them. We speak positively about them, sometimes ignoring their negative qualities or claiming they have fewer of these than they really do. For many people, this positive outlook is the most important part of friendship – being a 'good' friend is a matter of thinking and feeling positively about them, as well as acting in caring ways towards them.

This type of friendship is what I'll call 'knowledge-free' – it involves no requirement to really know or understand the other person. On the flip side, this view of friendship suggests that having negative beliefs about your friends (even if those beliefs are justified) makes you a worse friend. As someone who has researched friendship and goodness, this view of friendship just doesn't seem right to me. It doesn't capture all of what we want from friendship. I have studied the work of British-Irish novelist and philosopher Iris Murdoch – and I would argue that her writings provide us with a fuller view of friendship.

Iris Murdoch is known for her writing on morality, good and evil, and human relationships. She was interested in the reality of 'the Good' in an era when such theorising was deeply unpopular. A highly successful novelist, Murdoch's many books explore the challenges and problems of close relationships. Much of Murdoch's philosophical work examines the moral significance of love (which I consider to be part of friendship). She regarded love as a central part of our moral life that had been unreasonably ignored in the moral philosophy of her time.

Unlike the view of friendship I described earlier, Murdoch did not think of love as 'knowledge-free'. Instead, she suggested that understanding the other person is an integral part of love (and therefore of friendship, too). Murdoch's view of love is knowledge of the other person, or seeing them as they really are – it means understanding them as a person, both their positive and negative qualities. Notably, Murdoch thought that really knowing or understanding another person is a difficult task: 'It is a task to come to see the world as it is.' Murdoch agreed with psychologists who say that humans tend to be attracted to 'fantasy' – refusing to face the truth because it threatens the way we prefer to see ourselves.

So while we may have a natural, selfish tendency to believe reassuring fantasies about the goodness of other people (especially our friends), true friendship requires us to be patient, kind and accepting of their negative qualities, too. Being a good friend to others thus involves what Murdoch calls 'loving attention': regarding them in a patient, caring way, and always trying to do justice to who they really are. In Murdoch's view of friendship, being a good friend involves knowing or understanding our friends more fully. Think about the way a friendship develops: one might initially know a few facts about a friend's interests, such as that they enjoy classical music. Over time, a good friend would not simply know that their friend enjoys classical music, but exactly what kind of music they like, what it is that they like about it, and the importance that it has in their life. This deepening understanding of the other person naturally leads to a more fulfilling friendship.

So how might Murdoch's idea of friendship relate to the other things we usually expect of friends, such as that they treat us well, and help us when we need it? Once we truly, lovingly see and understand another person, the right way to behave towards them will follow naturally. We won't have to ask ourselves things like 'Should I bother helping my friend who is in need?', because seeing their need will itself make us feel compelled to act rightly. Think about Iris Murdoch the next time a friend of yours does or says something you disagree with. Instead of ignoring their flaw or mistake, try to accept it as part of their whole – it may even strengthen your friendship.

14 UNIT 3 GETTING ALONG

1 What is the writer doing in the first paragraph?
  A giving advice on how to maintain friendships
  B outlining what is often understood to constitute friendship
  C pointing out the most valuable aspects of friendship
  D explaining why kinder people form better friendships

2 What does the writer suggest about 'knowledge-free' friendship?
  A It should be avoided if at all possible.
  B It may end up making people more critical.
  C It is likely to leave people feeling dissatisfied.
  D It requires more effort than other relationships.

3 In the third paragraph, the writer says that Murdoch
  A regretted the widespread attitudes towards issues which she felt mattered.
  B feared that she was unable to make a meaningful contribution to philosophy.
  C acknowledged that her ideas would never become widespread in her lifetime.
  D accepted that focusing on a single feature of human behaviour was a mistake.

4 In the fourth paragraph, according to the writer, Murdoch believed that love
  A does not turn a person into someone who is kinder to others.
  B should not be thought of as an easy way to get to know another person.
  C may not be worth pursuing because it is so challenging for most people.
  D cannot exist between two people who imagine one another to be perfect.

5 Why does the writer mention classical music in the fifth paragraph?
  A to justify further discussion of friendship
  B to illustrate a point made about friendship
  C to demonstrate an advantage of friendship
  D to support a recommendation related to friendship

6 In the final paragraph, the writer implies that adopting Murdoch's approach to friendship
  A might encourage us to make more friends.
  B can be a positive way of resolving arguments.
  C has the potential to improve our relationships.
  D could lead to our questioning our own actions.

Part 4

2 **Look at the exam task and answer these questions about each item.**

1 Is the key word part of an idiom?
2 Which part(s) of the first sentence must you change?

✓ Exam task

3 For questions **1–6**, complete the second sentence so that it has a similar meaning to the first sentence, using the word given. **Do not change the word given.** You must use between **three** and **six** words, including the word given. Here is an example (**0**).

Example:

0 Sam has consistently attempted not to attract attention since the trial began.
  PROFILE
  Sam has made consistent ATTEMPTS TO KEEP A LOW PROFILE since the trial began.

1 I couldn't help laughing when my little cousin told me he was a faster runner than me.
  STRAIGHT
  I couldn't .... when my little cousin told me he was a faster runner than me.

2 My partner said I should remember to take my keys with me when I went out.
  LEAVE
  My partner reminded .... my keys behind when I went out.

3 While Jairo was abroad, he heard all the news about his home town from his friends.
  POSTED
  While Jairo was abroad, his friends kept .... that was happening in his home town.

4 The couple who adopted Julie knew her aunt and uncle very well.
  PARENTS
  Julie's .... friends of her aunt and uncle.

5 I hope you'll wish me well tomorrow when I have my job interview.
  FINGERS
  I hope you'll .... me tomorrow when I have my job interview.

6 The garage said someone would definitely repair my car by the end of the week.
  PROMISED
  The garage .... repaired by the end of the week.

UNIT 3 GETTING ALONG 15

Listening

Part 1

1 Look at the exam task and answer this question for each extract.

Who will you hear, and what will they talk about?

✓ **Exam task**

 2 🔊 04 You will hear three different extracts. For questions **1–6**, choose the answer (**A**, **B** or **C**) which fits best according to what you hear. There are two questions for each extract.

Extract One

You hear two friends discussing a two-week break they both took from social media.

1 What do they agree about the first week?
   A Time passed too slowly.
   B They felt a little isolated.
   C It was extremely challenging.

2 How does the woman feel now she's back on social media?
   A eager to share her experiences
   B overwhelmed by all the content
   C more self-confident than before

Extract Two

You hear part of an interview with a psychologist about some research into talking to strangers.

3 What does she say about the participants in the study?
   A Their personalities affected the outcome.
   B Their expectations of the interaction differed.
   C They were carefully selected by the researchers.

4 When talking about the implications of talking to strangers, the psychologist
   A warns that people's lives will not be dramatically altered.
   B admits the necessity for further research into the subject.
   C advises against interacting with people who do not look friendly.

Extract Three

You hear two people talking about getting back in touch with old friends after a long time.

5 When talking about contacting an old friend, the woman mentions her
   A relief at the response she received.
   B impatience at having to wait for a reply.
   C surprise about how nervous she initially was.

6 What does the man say about getting back in touch with childhood friends?
   A It should never feel like an obligation.
   B It is important to be cautious when doing so.
   C It may turn out to be less rewarding than anticipated.

Grammar

Reported speech

1 Choose the correct reporting verb in each sentence.

1 My little brother **refused** / **denied** taking the last piece of cake.
2 Louis **agreed** / **accepted** to help me fix my broken-down car.
3 Alex **threatened** / **warned** the children not to go into the pool straight after lunch.
4 Paola **offered** / **invited** to lend me her bicycle.
5 My sister **admitted** / **apologised** that she had lost my phone.
6 Juan **suggested** / **persuaded** everyone to go out for a walk.

2 Rewrite these statements as reported speech.

1 'I'll keep an eye out in case any interesting animals appear,' he said.
   He said ....
2 'I have some distant relatives in Portugal,' she said to me.
   She told ....
3 'I won't lose my cool,' he promised.
   He promised to ....
4 'Please look after my plants while I'm on holiday,' she said to her flatmate.
   She asked ....
5 'I didn't enjoy the film last night,' he said.
   He said ....
6 'I'm not looking for a long-term relationship,' she said to me.
   She informed ....

3 Rewrite these questions as reported speech.

1 'Do you always keep your word?' Saori asked me.
   Saori asked me ....
2 'Did you grow up in a close-knit family?' Frank asked me.
   Frank wanted to know ....
3 'Was the party fun?' Eric asked them.
   Eric asked them ....
4 'Where do you go to college?' Isabel asked him.
   Isabel asked him ....
5 'How long did it take you to get here?' Andres asked his sister.
   Andres wondered ....

UNIT 3 GETTING ALONG

Writing

Part 2 email

Register

1 The underlined words and phrases have been used by exam candidates in informal letters and emails. Replace these words and phrases with more appropriate informal alternatives and make any other changes necessary. (More than one answer may be possible.)

1 I regret not keeping my cool yesterday.
2 I've seen numerous films with that actor in it.
3 Silvio's busy tomorrow, thus cannot join us.
4 These persons don't really understand what it's like to be a teenager.
5 I have some tasks to execute before I go home.

2 Look at this exam task and answer these questions.

1 What problem has Jo got?
2 What does she want you to do?

 Exam task

This is part of an email you have received from an English-speaking friend.

> My younger brother is fourteen and he used to get on very well with my parents. But recently, he's been having loads of arguments with them, and family life has felt very uncomfortable. I love my brother and my parents. I'm really worried, and I want to help. Do you have any advice for me?
>
> Write back soon!
>
> Jo

Write your **email** in reply in **220–260** words.

3 Read the model email. In which paragraph(s) does the writer ...

1 give Jo some advice?
2 encourage Jo to keep in touch?
3 reassure Jo?

> Hi Jo,
>
> Thanks for your email. It was great to hear from you after all this time. **(1)** *But* I'm sorry to hear about the **(2)** *issues your family is encountering*. One thing I can say straight away is that it sounds very normal to me! **(3)** *One cannot conclude that* your family has suddenly become totally dysfunctional, or anything like that. This kind of thing happens in lots of families at one time or another. **(4)** *It's certainly happened* in mine!
>
> You don't say what the arguments are about, but I don't suppose that really matters. When I was your brother's age, my parents **(5)** *could frequently be a source of irritation*, about almost anything at all! So try not to worry too much. It does sound as if your brother and your parents need to talk about things, though. It isn't your responsibility, **(6)** *of course*, but it's affecting you, **(7)** *therefore it is in your own interest to do* something about it. One idea might be to ask them all to sit down together to discuss some of the things they disagree about. **(8)** *Are your parents likely to view this suggestion in a positive light*? Or perhaps you could ask someone in your extended family to have a chat with your brother about what's going on?
>
> Whatever **(9)** *the outcome*, let me know. And don't leave it so long to email me next time! Even if my suggestions aren't much good, maybe it'll help a bit to chat to me about it all from time to time.
>
> **(10)** *Take care*,
>
> Eli

4 Read the informal email again and look at the words and phrases in italics. Which ones are in an appropriate register and which ones should be replaced by words in the box below?

> Best regards   Do you think your parents would be OK with this?
> happens   However,   It doesn't mean   needless to say
> it has undoubtedly been the case   often got on my nerves
> problems your family is having   so it's worth doing

 Exam task

5 This is part of an email you have received from an English-speaking friend.

> ... Two new students have joined my Spanish class. They know each other well and laugh a lot together during the lessons. When the teacher puts us into groups to have a conversation, they do most of the talking, whether they're together or split up. I really like our teacher, but I don't think he's actually realised how it's making some of us feel. I'd like to do something about it, but I'm not sure what. I don't want to embarrass the teacher. Do you have any ideas?
>
> Thanks,
>
> Stevie

Write your **email** in reply in **220–260** words.

UNIT 3 GETTING ALONG   17

4 Making ends meet

Reading and Use of English
Part 7

✓ **Exam task**

1 You are going to read an article about a business academy for young people. Six paragraphs have been removed from the article. Choose from paragraphs **A–G** the one which fits each gap (**1–6**). There is one extra paragraph which you do not need to use.

The Enterprise Academy

Despite passing all his exams with top grades, 19-year-old Harry Day wasn't keen on the idea of academic study. He dropped out of school after one year of doing courses in maths, further maths, physics and chemistry to pursue a one-year course in Business and Enterprise at the Peter Jones Enterprise Academy at Solihull College.

1

The academy aims to give young people the skills they need to be similarly successful, and run their own businesses via a range of entrepreneurship courses delivered at around 30 UK colleges around the country. Students learn how to put together a business plan, network, build a brand, attract and keep the best employees, and effectively market their business.

2

As 20-year-old Charlie Buckingham found out, this can be about making mistakes – and learning from them. He initially started a pet supplies business while studying at the academy, but it went bust. That is when he realised that if he wanted to build a successful company, it should be based on something he was passionate about.

3

'I learnt that if you want to succeed, you have to put yourself out there. A lot of people fall at the first hurdle, but the people who get the most out of the academy are the ones who get out of their comfort zone.' In five years, he plans to be offering coaching and consultancy across the UK and has no regrets about not going to university. 'I don't think you can learn business from a textbook. You just have to get your hands dirty and do it,' he says.

4

Another graduate who has benefitted from this process, Anil Gupta, started to hone his entrepreneurial skills in his teens. The son of small-business owners, he always had his eyes open for opportunities, even as a child. 'I was just fascinated with the idea of creating an enterprise, like my parents had done.' At the age of 13, having noticed that his friends were sneaking out of school to buy fizzy drinks, he started buying cans of cola in bulk and selling them during breaktimes.

5

After finishing school, where he had particularly enjoyed courses in business, 3D design and accounting, he was keen to gain some real knowledge of business, but he wasn't attracted to idea of being 'tied down' to a three-year university course. So when he heard about the Peter Jones Enterprise Academy at nearby Leicester College, he jumped at it. By far the best part of the one-year course was being tutored by young entrepreneur Rhys Woodfield.

6

Now Anil is working full time on his business and loving every minute. He has no regrets about not going down the university route. 'I'm making money, I'm happy with my business. I just want to keep on going and put all of my time, effort and energy into making it a success.'

UNIT 4 MAKING ENDS MEET

A 'The practical approach is the best way to build up business skills,' agrees Jan Hodges, Chief Executive of an education charity. 'Helping young people develop in this way – even if they don't end up setting up their own businesses – is so important. These are exactly the kind of skills employers are looking for.'

B But what really motivates him is the idea of helping others to start and run their own business. The academy, he believes, fills a gaping hole in the education market, even though only a minority of graduates become entrepreneurs.

C 'We adopt a "learning by doing" approach, with business masterclasses, enterprise competitions and work-experience placements. Students are assigned a mentor from the local business community and are encouraged to work on "real-life" business ideas,' says Alice Barnard, Chief Executive of the Peter Jones Enterprise Academy.

D 'I'd typically think in terms of what I wanted from my business, but he helped me change my mind-set to become much more customer-focused. He also helped me draw up a business plan, and put things into perspective in terms of what was important and what wasn't.'

E 'I did OK,' he says. 'But it didn't last long, and soon I was working on my next big plan.' He has lost count of the number of schemes he devised and abandoned over the years.

F Two years on, with investor funding, he's about to launch his own fashion label, which will specialise in suits and formal wear for young men. He expects it to break even within the first six months of trading. 'I feel like I've found my true calling in life,' he says.

G So, building on his experience of working with young people, he set up his company Altruist Enterprises and now provides training to businesses and organisations to help them support employees with mental health issues.

Part 2

☑ **Exam task**

2 For questions **1–8**, read the text below and think of the word which best fits each gap. Use only **one** word in each gap. There is an example at the beginning (**0**).

Example: (**0**) BY

The people giving away 10% of their income

A (**0**) .... no means insignificant number of people have decided to give away 10% of their income for the rest of their working lives. They have joined an organisation (**1**) .... mission is to encourage its members to give this money to charities. A calculator on the organisation's site shows members the extent to (**2**) .... their 10% donation can have an impact. The organisation also publishes a list of all the donors. According to members, making a public commitment to donate not only helps them to live up (**3**) .... their own values, but also inspires others.

(**4**) .... this being a big commitment, members say they feel it is the right thing to do. They say they have comfortable lives and their needs are met, and they have (**5**) .... desire to keep on buying bigger and better cars, for example, let (**6**) .... spend a lot of money on (**7**) .... everyday luxuries as takeaway meals. They prefer to contribute towards tackling social injustice, and to show solidarity with people far (**8**) .... affluent than themselves.

Vocabulary

Money

1 Complete these sentences with words or phrases related to money. The first and last letter of each word are given.

1 I try to avoid my bank account being o _ _ _ _ _ _ _ n, so I don't have to pay i _ _ _ _ _ _ t.

2 Parts of this city are very p _ _ _ _ _ _ _ _ s, but in some less w _ _ _-o _ f areas, many of the businesses have gone b _ _ _ _ _ _ t.

3 After my g _ _ _ s income has been t _ _ _ d, I barely have enough left to c _ _ _ r my basic expenses: it's really hard for me to m _ _ e e _ _ s m _ _ t.

4 After two years of making a l _ _ s, this business is finally b _ _ _ _ _ _ g e _ _ n.

5 Unless the company starts making some s _ _ _ _ _ s and builds up more f _ _ _ s, it will not be able to survive a time in the future when it may not be making a p _ _ _ _ t.

6 Those earrings are not only so expensive they're u _ _ _ _ _ _ _ _ _ _ e, but they're also a total r _ _-o _ f!

UNIT 4 MAKING ENDS MEET ▶ **19**

Grammar

Passive and causative verb forms

1 Complete the second sentence so that it has a similar meaning to the first sentence. Use a passive or causative form.

1. The cashpoint is closed for the time being because someone is repairing the cash dispenser.
   This cashpoint is closed for the time being because the cash dispenser ....

2. My grandfather always wanted someone to print a receipt for him before he left the shop.
   My grandfather always wanted to .... before he left the shop.

3. We may deduct a transaction fee from your account if you make a purchase with your credit card abroad.
   A transaction fee .... from your account if you make a purchase with your credit card abroad.

4. People have predicted that coins will become obsolete within a couple of years.
   Coins .... within a couple of years.

5. People often say that the world of high finance is a very fast-paced environment.
   It .... is a very fast-paced environment.

2 Correct the mistakes in these sentences.

1. A large number of the current problems is caused by other factors.
   ....

2. It took ages for us to get finally seated.
   ....

3. The minibus broke down and we waited for a couple of hours to get fixed.
   ....

4. She tried to let not get her hat blown away in the strong wind.
   ....

5. The landlord doesn't want anything in the house be damaged.
   ....

Listening

Part 3

✓ Exam task

1 🔊 05 You will hear part of an interview on a podcast in which two young people, Nola Deans and Lawrence Stevens, are discussing the subject of money. For questions **1–6**, choose the answer (**A**, **B**, **C** or **D**) which fits best according to what you hear.

1. What does Nola think about money in general?
   A It is unfairly distributed.
   B It should be worked for.
   C People care about it too much.
   D Having a lot of it can have a negative impact.

2. What does Lawrence say about saving money for the future?
   A People on low incomes cannot be expected to do so.
   B People are not encouraged to plan ahead financially.
   C People often avoid thinking about it until it is too late.
   D People his age consider that living well now matters more.

3. What is Nola's priority when managing her money?
   A covering her transport costs
   B paying for her accommodation
   C ensuring she has a nutritious diet
   D being able to have an active social life

4. When talking about advertising, Nola and Lawrence agree that it
   A has a negative influence on society.
   B is frequently deliberately misleading.
   C can draw attention to useful products.
   D provides vital funding for many websites.

5. How do Nola and Lawrence both say they feel when donating money to charity?
   A proud to be assisting others
   B embarrassed to be giving so little
   C grateful that it is affordable for them
   D concerned about how the money will be spent

6. What does Lawrence predict about his finances?
   A He will be able to pay off his debts.
   B Buying a flat will remain unaffordable.
   C Getting a better paid job will be difficult.
   D He will enjoy a more comfortable lifestyle.

20 UNIT 4 MAKING ENDS MEET

Writing

Part 1 essay

1 Read the exam task and model essay, ignoring the gaps, and answer these questions.

1 Which two benefits have been written about?
2 How have these benefits been paraphrased?
3 What is given as the most important reason for children to learn about money?

✅ Exam task

Your class has had a discussion on teaching young children, from around the age of five, about money. You have made the notes below.

> **Benefits for young children of being taught about money**
> - understanding the value of money
> - developing the ability to wait for a reward
> - learning about the consequences of their choices

> Some opinions expressed in the discussion:
> 'Spending pocket money teaches what money can buy.'
> 'It's good to learn to save up for things.'
> 'Buying sweets now may mean you can't afford something else later.'

Write an essay for your teacher discussing **two** of the benefits in your notes. You should **explain which is the most important reason why young children should be taught about money, giving reasons** to support your opinion.

You may, if you wish, make use of the opinions expressed in the discussion, but you should use your own words as far as possible.

3 Which of the words in the box below could replace each gapped addition link? More than one answer is possible in some cases, and the words in the box can be used more than once.

> besides   finally   firstly   furthermore   lastly
> moreover   most importantly   secondly

✅ Exam task

4 Your class has had a discussion on the idea of a universal basic income: giving all adult citizens of a country a fixed amount of money every month to cover their basic costs, regardless of how much money they already have. You have made the notes below.

> **Benefits of having a universal basic income**
> - Everyone could afford to eat healthily.
> - People could take time away from work to improve their skills.
> - Parents could choose whether or not to stay at home.

> Some opinions expressed in the discussion:
> 'Nutritious food is often expensive.'
> 'Better qualifications often lead to more satisfying jobs.'
> 'It's good for people with young children to be able to have a few months off work.'

Write an essay for your teacher discussing **two** of the benefits in your notes. You should **explain which you think would be the main advantage for people of having a universal basic income, giving reasons** to support your opinion.

You may, if you wish, make use of the opinions expressed in the discussion, but you should use your own words as far as possible.

Write your **essay** in **220–260** words in an appropriate style.

2 Complete each gap in the essay with one word.

It is said that money makes the world go round, and learning to spend money wisely and save for the future are often seen as vital life skills. Teaching children from an early age how to deal with money would seem, therefore, to be worth undertaking.

(1) .... the first place, discovering what can be purchased with a particular sum of money is something that everyone needs to become aware of at some point. So, it appears reasonable to start teaching children this from an early age. A simple way of doing so is giving them a small amount of cash every week and taking them to shops in order to allow them to see for themselves what can be acquired with it.

What (2) .... more, learning about money can be another means of introducing another invaluable concept, namely the future impact of decisions made today. If, for example, a child chooses to spend all their money on a toy they really want, they may regret it later when they come across something even more desirable, but no longer have any money left to buy it with.

In my view, the sooner children become conscious of the link between actions and their implications, the better. Consequently, I see this as the most important reason for teaching them about money. For (3) .... start, it not only matters when it comes to money, but in many other areas of life, too. (4) .... addition, it should develop their capacity for logical reasoning. Above (5) .... , it encourages them to take responsibility for their own decisions.

UNIT 4 MAKING ENDS MEET   21

5 Well-being and sport

Reading and Use of English
Part 8

1 Before doing the exam task, underline the key words or phrases in the questions.

How to sleep better

A Many of us are hoping for a happier, healthier life. We may already have tried lifestyle changes (for example daily meditation, giving up dairy), but for most of us the greatest gains to be had are in sleeping better. Regardless of your specific goal, it's hard to achieve anything when you've had insufficient sleep. On the flipside, everything seems more possible when you're well rested. Sleep boosts your ability to fight infections, regulates mood and digestion, and can make you more productive, patient or creative. It sharpens the mind and can prolong your life. 'Sleep is one of the most powerful things you can do for your body. It's just critical to make that a priority,' says Aric Prather, psychologist and professor of psychiatry and behavioural sciences. 'The more work you put into it, the better you'll sleep.' The aims of Prather's practice are to regulate our internal clock and to address any anxieties or hangups we've developed around sleep.

B It may be that, without realising it, you've formed bedtime habits that promote wakefulness; but before you can change your behaviour, you must become conscious of it. Prather asks the patients at his sleep clinic to start keeping a handwritten 'sleep diary', recording facts such as how long it took them to fall asleep, the number of times they woke during the night, their wake-up time and estimated sleep quality. The aim is to highlight patterns and possible areas for improvement. 'Sleep is universal, but it's also really personal,' says Prather. The diary is the first step towards an approach that will work for you. Often Prather's patients have had one 'terrible' night, and worry about it happening again. They may go to bed early to make up for it, then lie there worrying that sleep won't come, which worsens their insomnia. Accepting that falling asleep will sometimes be impossible, for reasons outside your control, helps to relieve the stress, frustration and anxiety around it, perhaps making you more likely to succeed.

C If you're struggling to sleep, it's tempting to 'catch up' by sleeping late at the weekends or when you can, but this can actually further confuse our internal 'drivers' of sleep, says Prather. 'Our brain is always taking on information, trying to keep us alive, making predictions about what's going to happen next – so the more things can be stable and consistent, the better those predictions are. Trying to go to bed at the same time every night can pile on pressure that isn't helpful for sleep', he continues. Instead, he advises waking up at the same time (or within a half-hour window) every day to regulate your circadian rhythm, which governs your bodily processes and whether you are a night owl or an early bird. What time you choose is up to you, says Prather; the key is to keep it the same. If it's a challenge to begin with, he suggests linking it with something that you look forward to, such as making a delicious breakfast. After a while, you should naturally start to feel sleepy around the same time every night.

D Your brain needs time to relax after the pressures of the day and prepare you for sleep – if possible, about two hours before your ideal bedtime. Often people treat their brains and their bodies like laptops: 'Well, turn it off!' advises Prather. 'I wish it was that way ... but we need to have an adequate transition.' The ideal post-work, pre-bed activity will be different for everybody: some people listen to podcasts, others might write a diary or do some gentle stretching. These routines can become environmental triggers, encouraging us to shift gears into sleep. Even television can help us wind down, says Prather (though he advises against watching it in bed). However, he adds, there's a big difference between starting a nail-biting new drama and relaxing with old episodes of a familiar show. Similarly, the anxiety-inducing content of your social media timeline is probably more harmful to sleep than the blue light being emitted by your phone. If, after two hours, you're still wide awake, it could be that your bedtime routine is too stimulating. Prather recommends meditating instead, or listening to gentle music.

✅ Exam task

2 You are going to read an article about sleep. For questions **1–10**, choose from the four sections (**A–D**). The sections may be chosen more than once.

Which section contains

1 an observation that occasional nights without sleep are inevitable?
2 a scientific term for what influences exactly when people feel most active and awake?
3 a claim that there is a direct link between effort and rewards?
4 reasons why getting extra sleep may have the opposite effect to that intended?
5 examples of how some choices are worse than others?
6 a warning that improved sleep relies on an awareness of obstacles to it?
7 a recommendation to help those reluctant to adopt a routine?
8 a description of a process which individuals are requested to engage in?
9 a comment on how essential sleep is for enhanced well-being?
10 advice against expecting something to occur instantly?

Part 3

Vocabulary – Suffixes

3 Find words in the questions and text in the Reading Part 8 task on page 22 which are formed from the following words.

a harm (noun, verb) ....
b anxious (adjective) ....
c predict (verb) ....
d nature (noun) ....
e frustrated (adjective) ....
f aware (adjective) ....
g psychology (noun) ....
h instant (noun, adjective) ....

4 What part of speech are the words you found? Which suffixes are used in these words to form nouns, verbs, adjectives and adverbs?

5 Use the word in capitals to form a word that fits in the gap in each sentence.

1 Facing up to difficult situations is a .... thing to do. COURAGE
2 This basketball arena has a seating .... of 20,000. CAPABLE
3 The children played table tennis very ....! ENTHUSIASM
4 The tennis player showed great .... of character to beat his opponent after he nearly lost the match. STRONG
5 I could never dive into the sea from such a great ....! HIGH

6 Look at the exam task and decide which part of speech is needed in each gap. If a noun is needed, should it be singular or plural?

✅ Exam task

7 For questions **1–8**, read the text below. Use the word given in capitals at the end of some of the lines to form a word that fits in the gap **in the same line**. There is an example at the beginning (**0**).

Write your answers **IN CAPITAL LETTERS**.

Example: (**0**) MOVEMENTS

The Paralympic Games

The word 'Paralympic' derives from the Greek preposition 'para' (beside or alongside) and the word 'Olympic', illustrating how the Paralympic and Olympic
(**0**) .... exist side by side. **MOVE**

Sport for athletes with
(**1**) .... has been around **ABLE**
for a long time. In 1888 in Berlin,
the first sports clubs for the deaf
were already in (**2**) .... **EXIST**
It was not until after 1945, however,
that such sports became
(**3**) .... Their purpose **SPREAD**
was to provide support for the large
number of people wounded during
World War II, many of whom faced
great (**4**) .... **HARD**

In 1944, Dr Ludwig Guttmann
opened a (**5**) .... **SPINE**
injuries centre at Stoke Mandeville
Hospital in England. The games
played there for (**6**) .... **THERAPY**
purposes gradually evolved into
competitive sports. In 1952, the
International Stoke Mandeville
Games were founded, attracting
many participants who were
(**7**) .... gifted. These **EXCEPTION**
games subsequently became
the Paralympic Games, first held
in 1960 in Rome, Italy, featuring
400 (**8**) .... from 23 **CONTEST**
countries. Since then, they have
taken place every four years. In
1976, the first Winter Paralympics
were held in Sweden.

UNIT 5 WELL-BEING AND SPORT

Listening
Part 2

1 Read sentences 1–8 below in the exam task and think about the kind of information which is missing and what part of speech is likely to fill each gap.

✓ **Exam task**

2 🔊 06 You will hear a man called David Alegretti giving a talk to a group of fellow students about swimming in an outdoor pool.

For questions **1–8**, complete the sentences with a word or short phrase.

Swimming in an outdoor pool

David hoped to improve his
(1) .... by taking up swimming.
When David arrived at the pool, he was sent to a (2) .... to get changed in.
During David's first swim, he saw a
(3) .... running into the woods nearby.
David says it requires a great deal of
(4) .... to get up early to go swimming.
David explains that (5) ....
is the style of swimming he has made most progress in.
David uses the words
(6) .... to describe swimming outdoors.
David has (7) .... for breakfast after his morning swim.
David says it feels as if his
(8) .... have grown larger.

Grammar
Conditional forms

1 Put the verbs in brackets into the correct form to complete the sentences.

1 Even if the best player in your team .... (not break) her arm last week, you .... (not be) likely to beat the team at the top of the league tomorrow.
2 As long as you .... (take) the correct dose, this medicine .... (do) you no harm.
3 Supposing we .... (go) online really early tomorrow, do you think we .... (be) able to book a badminton court?
4 Unless you .... (leave) right now, you .... (not get) to the stadium on time.
5 Assuming I .... (tell) you before the race last week that I felt dizzy, ... (you let) me take part?
6 .... (she have) a better life now if she .... (not give up) her dreams of becoming an Olympic champion?

2 Complete each sentence so that it means what is indicated above it.

1 stay dry now → not feel cold later
   Provided you ....
2 I did my physiotherapy exercises → knee better now
   If I ....
3 all cars electric → the air much cleaner
   Imagine that all ....
4 you must be over 21 → take part in this clinical trial
   On condition that ....
5 she followed medical advice → she recovered
   Had ....

UNIT 5 WELL-BEING AND SPORT

Writing

Part 2 proposal

Purpose and reason links

1 Choose the correct linking words or phrases in these sentences.

1 My sister worked very hard **so that** / **in order to** make it as a surgeon.
2 The council will evaluate what is already available **so as to** / **in order that** make an informed decision.
3 Leon went outside **so that** / **in order** he could breathe some fresh air.
4 Do some exercise after studying all day if you can, **in order not to** / **to not** get too unfit.
5 Kieran is seeing a therapist **so** / **to** learn to deal better with setbacks.
6 The college is taking measures **so as not to** / **in order to not** put students at risk.
7 The gym will close early **in order that** / **in order to** the heating can be fixed by tomorrow.
8 The sports centre opening hours are being extended **in order for** / **so as to** more people to be able to exercise there.

2 Read the exam task. What ideas would you suggest if you were going to write this proposal?

✅ Exam task

You are studying English in an English-speaking country. You see this announcement on the local town council website.

> The town council are looking for ideas to improve the well-being of people in this town. We would like to invite anyone living or staying here to send us a proposal giving us your ideas, suggesting how the town council could implement them and telling us why they would benefit local people.

Write your **proposal** in **220–260** words in an appropriate style.

3 Read the section headings for the model proposal. Are any of the ideas similar to yours?

1 Introduction
2 A community garden
3 Cookery classes
4 Group walks
5 Conclusion

4 Look at sections A–E. Which section goes under each heading in Exercise 3?

A
Not everyone nowadays prepares nutritious meals at home. Because of this, some people develop health problems which might otherwise be avoided. If the council were to set up workshops or short courses to teach citizens about healthy ingredients and how to use them in dishes, many individuals and families would have better diets.

B
I very much hope that the council will consider my recommendations and take measures to implement them as soon as is practically possible.

C
The purpose of this proposal is to make suggestions to help increase the well-being of local people.

D
Currently, a relatively large section of the town's population does not take much exercise outdoors. The council could organise outings for local people to join on foot, and provide staff to lead these. If the trips were to take place not only during the week but also at weekends, working people and retired people would all have the opportunity to take part. It is well-known that contact with nature is good for both mental and physical health, and this would therefore be a positive step.

E
Many people in this town live in apartments, and it is not uncommon for these to have no balconies. Consequently, a significant number of inhabitants have no access to an outdoor space. If the council were to set aside a small area of land for everyone to use to grow flowers and vegetables, this would provide opportunities for local people, young and old, to meet and do something productive and enjoyable together.

5 Look at sections 2–4. Have the requirements of the exam task been addressed in each case?

✅ Exam task

6 You see this announcement on your English college website.

> The College Management wants to encourage students at the college to do more exercise. This could be sports or physical activity more generally. Please write a proposal suggesting what the college could do, and how your ideas would benefit students at the college.

Write your **proposal** in an appropriate style in **220–260** words.

UNIT 5 WELL-BEING AND SPORT 25

6 Art and entertainment

Reading and Use of English
Part 5

✓ **Exam task**

1 You are going to read an article about a TV show. For questions **1–6**, choose the answer (**A**, **B**, **C**, or **D**) which you think fits best according to the text.

An unusual piano competition

Reporter Michael Hogan talked to the presenter and judges of a TV talent show.

The TV contest *The Piano* is a search for undiscovered keyboard talent which is based on the 'street piano' phenomenon. Over the past few years, come-and-have-a-go instruments have appeared in stations, shopping centres and other public spaces. People passing by are encouraged to either sit down and play, or stop and listen. Smiling crowds, cheerful commutes and viral videos have resulted. The presenter of the show, Claudia Winkleman, invites gifted amateurs to perform at four of the UK's busiest stations, before a sensational plot twist: unbeknown to the participants, this isn't a documentary – it's a competition. They're secretly being judged by two globally famous musical talents: classical pianist Lang Lang and pop star Mika, who choose the best contestants to play to an audience of thousands in a concert during the final episode of the show.

Both Mika and Lang Lang are hugely successful artists who sell out concerts pretty much anywhere. What persuaded them to take part for – as the series creator himself admits – 'not much money'? Eagerness to spread the word about the piano. 'TV has never really had a piano competition accessible to everyone,' says Lang Lang. 'We've had professional contests or series for vocalists, but never just piano. This instrument really is for everybody. Piano connects people, it touches hearts. This is the sort of show I've always wanted to do.'

For Mika, the attraction was the show's sweetness, and the sincerity and honesty of the producers. 'The concept was quite pure,' he says. 'It's so refreshing to talk about music and musicians without the stereotypical 15-minutes-of-fame approach of every other TV contest.' Avoiding sob stories doesn't mean *The Piano* lacks emotion. Every episode has several moments when the audience is likely to be brought to tears – at times through laughter, at others through sadness.

The Piano's contestants are hugely diverse, with ages spanning from six to 95. They play jazz, pop, classical, boogie-woogie, hip-hop, even electronic dance music favourites. Some opt for classical repertoire or songbook standards, others their own compositions. Some let their fingers do the talking, others sing or rap on top. What the judges are looking for is passion, personality and pure technique. As Lang Lang says: 'Whether it's a little kid or an octogenarian, I want to feel their soul and learn their story. Many pianists play very well technically, but it's mechanical.' 'Amateurs bring honesty,' adds Mika. 'They wear their heart on their sleeve in a way professionals just aren't able to do.'

Key to *The Piano's* format is the element of surprise. Playing in train stations rather than concert halls reflects this, making the whole atmosphere much more casual and unpredictable. It also provides a dramatic conclusion to each episode, as Winkleman gathers the players to reveal the truth, before bringing out the judges to announce their winner. 'They have no idea they're being watched,' says Winkleman. While making the show, she says she was wowed at every turn. 'It's extraordinary how a pianist can move a whole station. People are racing to work or rushing off on holiday. Children are crying, parents are stressed. But a pianist can just bring everything to a standstill. They sit down and make time stop. It's incredibly powerful.' Lang Lang agrees: 'In a train station, people come and go, but when the magic happens, suddenly the crowd stays.'

Shooting the show did involve quite a lot of challenges. Station announcements would interrupt performances. 'Somebody lost their bag, so I ran around trying to find this pink rucksack. A couple had an argument which I tried to solve but actually made worse. All that was happening around us – but that's the magic of street pianos,' says Winkleman. According to Lang Lang, the programme 'shows the sheer joy of music, no matter who you are.' 'I hope Lang Lang is right,' says Mika. 'The show is a reminder that a train station isn't a cold place, just like the country isn't a cold place. When people stop rushing around and come together through music, everything feels a bit kinder.'

UNIT 6 ART AND ENTERTAINMENT

1 What does the writer suggest about the show in the first paragraph?
   A Large numbers of people were encouraged to watch while it was being recorded.
   B The concept that inspired it is less original than many viewers might initially think.
   C Its appeal is partly due to the fact that participants are deceived about their role in it.
   D Players could only be selected for it if they had been heard performing in a public place.

2 According to the second paragraph, Mika and Lang Lang are mainly motivated by a desire to
   A enhance the popularity of the piano among the general public.
   B explore the way the piano brings people together.
   C provide insights into what playing the piano feels like.
   D recreate for TV the thrill of hearing high-quality live piano playing.

3 What is implied about TV contests in the third paragraph?
   A Their format does not tend to be particularly innovative.
   B The funny side of situations is only occasionally included.
   C They rarely enable the participants to become really well-known.
   D Those who make them do not always have very good intentions.

4 What is suggested about the contestants in the fourth paragraph?
   A Their lack of expertise can in fact be a positive feature.
   B Some of them adopt an unusual approach to piano playing.
   C Finding a wide variety of non-professionals was easier than expected.
   D They are all so different that it can be hard to evaluate their performances.

5 What is emphasised in the fifth paragraph?
   A how significant a role a presenter can play
   B how intense an impact musicians can have
   C how alert to their surroundings some travellers can be
   D how demanding it can be to perform in certain settings

6 One problem associated with filming the show was
   A the interfering attitude of railway officials.
   B the inevitable distractions due to the location.
   C having to do everything more rapidly than usual.
   D members of the public objecting to the disruption.

Part 1

2 Read the text of the exam task quickly, ignoring the gaps. Then, before you look at the options, try to think of a word which could fit in each gap.

✓ Exam task

3 For questions **1–8**, read the text below and decide which answer (**A**, **B**, **C** or **D**) best fits each gap. There is an example at the beginning (**0**).

Example:

0 **A** completely **B** totally **C** genuinely **D** certainly

Photography: is it art?

Can photography (0)  be regarded as art? Many early photographers (1) .... on paintings for inspiration, and some recognised straight away that photographs often have to be carefully composed, lit and produced. And when the 19th-century photographer Henry Fox Talbot published his thoughts on photography in the first book to contain photographic illustrations, he entitled it *The Pencil of Nature*.

(2) ...., for nearly 200 years, the (3) .... that photography was not actually art is something that photographers (4) .... came up against. At an early meeting of the Photographic Society of London, established in 1853, one member complained that the new technique could not compete with works of art on the (5) .... that it was unable to 'elevate the imagination'. Even by the 1970s, the idea that photographs could (6) .... more than simply surface appearances was not (7) .... acknowledged.

However, in 2011, the debate was effectively (8) .... when Andreas Gursky's photograph of a grey river Rhine under an equally colourless sky sold for a world-record price of £2.7 million.

1 **A** called   **B** looked   **C** drew   **D** based
2 **A** Otherwise   **B** Nonetheless **C** Besides   **D** Though
3 **A** demand   **B** report   **C** expression **D** claim
4 **A** repeatedly **B** drastically **C** immensely **D** intensively
5 **A** grounds   **B** condition   **C** evidence   **D** argument
6 **A** secure   **B** catch   **C** engage   **D** capture
7 **A** utterly   **B** widely   **C** deeply   **D** highly
8 **A** agreed   **B** decided   **C** settled   **D** confirmed

UNIT 6 ART AND ENTERTAINMENT   27

Listening

Part 4

✓ Exam task

 1 🔊 07 You will hear five short extracts in which people are talking about being part of an amateur drama group.

While you listen, you must complete both tasks.

TASK ONE

For questions **1–5**, choose from the list (**A–H**) why each speaker joined an amateur drama group.

A to fulfil an ambition
B to share some insights
C to broaden their horizons
D to overcome shyness
E to brush up on some skills
F to help them unwind
G to accompany an acquaintance
H to bounce back after a difficult time

Speaker 1 [1]
Speaker 2 [2]
Speaker 3 [3]
Speaker 4 [4]
Speaker 5 [5]

TASK TWO

For questions **6–10**, choose from the list (**A–H**) how each speaker felt about the group at first.

A It was competently run.
B Commitment was required from members.
C It provided a supportive environment.
D The standard of acting was very high.
E Some members were harsh critics.
F Its objectives were very idealistic.
G The plays were thoughtfully chosen.
H The atmosphere was competitive.

Speaker 1 [6]
Speaker 2 [7]
Speaker 3 [8]
Speaker 4 [9]
Speaker 5 [10]

Grammar

Verbs followed by the infinitive and/or -ing

1 Choose the correct verb forms to complete the sentences.

1 She remembers **catch / to catch / catching** a glimpse of a famous celebrity when she was at the opera.
2 He's trying **build / to build / building** a career as a portrait artist.
3 I don't regret **devote / to devote / devoting** so much of my life to art!
4 During our walk, we stopped **look / to look / looking** at some historical buildings.
5 Missing the bus meant **have / to have / having** to walk to the museum.
6 If you forget **renew / to renew / renewing** your season ticket on time, you may have to pay extra.
7 My parents didn't let me **walk / to walk / walking** to choir rehearsal on my own.
8 Is it worth **go / to go / going** to see that play at the local theatre?

2 Put the verb in brackets into the correct form to complete each sentence.

1 I regret .... (inform) you that the concert has been cancelled.
2 I don't think I'll ever forget .... (meet) Angelica for the first time.
3 He caught the actor .... (read) his lines from a note.
4 It's better to ask a question than pretend .... (understand) something you don't.
5 They suggested .... (leave) for the show an hour earlier than planned.
6 It's not worth .... (try) to book a table in that restaurant – it's always full.

3 Complete the second sentence so it has a similar meaning to the first.

1 Please close the door!
   Remember ....
2 I hope he continues to play the guitar when he's older.
   I hope he doesn't stop ....
3 He upset the director, but it wasn't his intention.
   He didn't mean ....
4 Maybe if you use better glue, you'll be able to fix that vase.
   Maybe you should try ....
5 Going to that rock concert is too expensive for me.
   I can't afford ....
6 My art teacher won't take us to that exhibition.
   My art teacher refuses ....
7 If you sing that line again and again, your song will improve.
   If you practise ....
8 Could you use your headphones to practise the piano, please?
   Would you mind ....?

28 UNIT 6 ART AND ENTERTAINMENT

Writing
Part 2 review

1 Put the words and phrases for describing films, books, TV shows, computer games, etc. into the correct columns in the table below.

> appalling   captivating   convincing   distinctive
> fast-paced   hilarious   imaginative
> inspiring   monotonous   much-anticipated
> outstanding   overrated   pointless   puzzling
> tedious   timeless   unconventional   wordy

positive	negative	neutral

2 Read this exam task and the model review, ignoring the adverbs in bold. Do you think you would prefer the book or the film?

✓ Exam task

> You see this announcement in an international magazine.
>
> > Books have often been turned into films, with varying degrees of success. We'd like our readers' opinions!
> > Send us a review of a film you have seen based on a book you enjoyed. Compare the film to the original book and tell us whether you think the adaptation is successful. Who would you recommend the film to?
> > The best reviews will be published next month in our magazine.
>
> Write your **review**.

Pride and Prejudice

As a teenager, I read one of Jane Austen's most popular novels, *Pride and Prejudice*. It is rightly regarded, in my opinion, as a timeless classic and I found it **(1) absolutely / eagerly** gripping. I was therefore a little reluctant to watch the recent much-anticipated film version of the novel, fearing that it might be **(2) widely / deeply** disappointing.

Despite my low expectations, the film was **(3) completely / highly** entertaining, fast-paced and at times, **(4) totally / dreadfully** hilarious. The dialogue, often taken straight from the novel, is as **(5) wonderfully / totally** witty as you would expect of Austen's distinctive style. I found the acting convincing, and some of the settings were spectacular, too.

Inevitably, the film version cannot portray all the inner thoughts of the characters. I missed the insights given to the reader by Austen's outstanding writing, the feeling that although she died over 200 years ago, she was speaking directly to me. However, the subtle interactions between the characters are often **(6) generally / perfectly** conveyed, thanks to some excellent acting. I even enjoyed watching the **(7) highly / dreadfully** pretentious Caroline Bingley!

This film will appeal to any teenager or adult who loves a good story. It may not be action-packed and there are no superheroes, but if you want proof that human beings can be remarkably similar across time and across cultures, this is a film you will appreciate. However, if you possibly can, read the novel, too. You are likely to be **(8) utterly / perfectly** captivated!

3 Now choose the correct intensifying adverb for each adjective in the model review.

✓ Exam task

4 You see this notice on an international film website.

> Would you like to contribute a review for our series 'Children's films from around the world'?
> Send us a review of two children's films you have seen. Compare and contrast the two films and tell us what kind of children might enjoy them.
> The best reviews will appear on our website.

Write your **review** in 220–260 words in an appropriate style.

UNIT 6 ART AND ENTERTAINMENT

7 Green living

Reading and Use of English

Part 7

✓ Exam task

1 You are going to read a newspaper article about a type of seaweed called kelp. Six paragraphs have been removed from the article. Choose from the paragraphs **A–G** the one which fits each gap (**1–6**). There is one extra paragraph which you do not need to use.

Giant kelp forests

Bubbles stream up behind Frank Hurd as he gently parts the curtains of giant kelp. Green and gold ribbons reach upwards through the cold waters of the Pacific Ocean towards the sun. Hurd, a marine biologist, is diving in a kelp forest off the coast of southern California. The thick, healthy kelp – a type of seaweed – forms a small part of underwater forests that blanket the coastline of nearly every continent.

1

That is because despite being one of the fastest growing plants on Earth, kelp has historically been difficult to map because of the difficulties of measuring ocean depths with satellites. However, a group of scientists, including marine ecologist Dr Karen Filbee-Dexter, who decided to model the global distribution of these amazing plants, have discovered that seaweed forests are far more extensive than previously realised.

2

This is very good news, as seaweed forests can act as vital protection against the climate crisis, absorbing carbon dioxide from seawater and the atmosphere. Having this more accurate figure is helpful; they may store as much carbon as the Amazon rainforest, according to one analysis. Unlike other marine plants such as mangroves and seagrass, however, seaweed lacks a root system to lock carbon into the ground, and there is still a gap in our understanding of its ability to sequester carbon.

3

Another reason why kelp is important is that it is a crucial part of marine ecosystems. It is the largest seaweed species, able to grow tens of metres high. In Australia, native kelp is home to the weedy seadragon, a colourful creature which only lives along the country's coastline. Kelp forests along North America's Pacific coast are vital habitats for southern sea otters.

4

Underwater forests could also have another role, thanks to their rapid growth. Seaweed has been mass-consumed in Asia for centuries, and now Western markets are catching on, albeit on a small scale, with more European and North American companies manufacturing seaweed products for human consumption. Yet these underwater forests face multiple threats, including rising sea temperatures, pollution and invasive species.

5

Seaweed forests are often overlooked and less studied compared with coral reefs, making it difficult to understand how they are changing. 'Most of the world's seaweed forests are not even mapped, much less monitored,' says Dr Filbee-Dexter. While corals are found in warm, calm and easily accessible areas, making them fairly easy to study, kelp is in cold waters on some of the roughest coasts in the world. She believes that the more scientists understand about these vital but fragile marine ecosystems, the easier it will be to help them survive.

6

However, as science continues to develop smarter technologies to track kelp, such as drones, satellites and AI, there is hope that further research can shed light on the role of kelp in fighting climate breakdown. It seems that kelp should never be underestimated for the productivity and biodiversity it supports around the world, and should be protected and restored urgently.

A They searched through hundreds of studies, including local plant data records, online repositories and citizen science initiatives. Their efforts revealed that underwater forests cover between 6 and 7.2 million km^2, an area roughly twice the size of India.

B On the contrary, reef areas nearby are filled with marine life. This includes crabs, octopuses, and a wide variety of fish. The scientists are keen to record the different species and their numbers.

C In California, Hurd is doing what he can to add to this knowledge as he dives among the kelp forests, monitoring their progress and hoping their decline can be stemmed. 'The loss of these incredibly productive ecosystems is devastating for both nature and people,' he says.

D According to Dr Filbee-Dexter, the new research into the size and locations of kelp forests around the world will go a long way to making up for that knowledge deficit regarding their potential contribution. Indeed, a more complete picture of the spread of kelp will be key to determining the role it could play in reducing the rate of global warming.

E Along the northern California coast, for instance, kelp has declined by more than 95% over the past several years, eaten by sea urchins – whose population has exploded as vast numbers of starfish, their main predators, have been killed by a disease linked to warming waters. Kelp forests along stretches of Australia's southern coastline and in the north-west Atlantic, along the coasts of Maine, Canada and Greenland, are also showing concerning signs of decline.

F Some of them are relatively well-studied, including the Great African Sea Forest and the Great Southern Reef, a giant kelp forest off southern Australia. But many more are unnamed and unknown – hidden underwater.

G In addition, kelp forests provide shelter for grey whales hiding from predatory killer whales. They are also essential feeding grounds for their young during their migration to Alaskan waters from Baja California in Mexico.

Part 4

✓ Exam task

2 For questions **1–6**, complete the second sentence so that it has a similar meaning to the first sentence, using the word given. **Do not change the word given.** You must use between three and six words, including the word given. Here is an example (0).

Example:

0 Chantal was delighted to see that her bank was no longer investing in fossil fuels.

MOON

Chantal was ..... OVER THE MOON WHEN SHE ..... saw that her bank was no longer investing in fossil fuels.

1 Perhaps my attempts at being eco-friendly are relatively insignificant, but I still think they're worth pursuing.

DROP

My attempts at being eco-friendly may just ...., but I still think they're worth pursuing.

2 Ahmed has changed jobs and is now repairing offshore wind turbines.

TAKEN

Ahmed .... role, repairing offshore wind turbines.

3 Prioritising economic growth over everything else is taking a dangerous risk.

FIRE

It is .... prioritise economic growth over everything else.

4 When I heard the council suggest their renewable energy plan, it was great.

FORWARD

It was great to .... their renewable energy plan.

5 Can you tell me about life in your city?

LIKE

Can you tell me what .... live in your city?

6 I found her ideas for achieving a more sustainable lifestyle new and exciting.

BREATH

Her ideas for achieving a more sustainable lifestyle ...., in my opinion.

UNIT 7 GREEN LIVING 31

Listening

Part 1

Vocabulary – Environment

1 Match words from List A with words from List B to make two-word phrases. Write a sentence using each phrase.

A	carbon	consumer	ecological	greenhouse	life	net
B	expectancy	gas	goods	impact	neutral	zero

✓ Exam task

2 🔊 08 You will hear three different extracts. For questions **1–6**, choose the answer (**A**, **B** or **C**) which fits best according to what you hear. There are two questions for each extract.

Extract One

You hear two colleagues discussing the new solar panels on their office block.

1 What had the woman assumed about the owners of the building?
   A They would not want to invest in solar energy.
   B They would not bother to implement the project.
   C They would not have the installation done properly.

2 They both think that having the panels
   A makes the workers in their office feel good.
   B will have a significant environmental impact.
   C sets a positive example for the neighbourhood.

Extract Two

You hear part of an interview with a climate scientist.

3 How does he feel about his work?
   A frustrated at its limitations
   B confident that he is in the right field
   C surprised by how his career has developed

4 What does he say about plastic waste?
   A Focusing on it as an issue may be a mistake.
   B Adults are less concerned about it than children.
   C Most governments accept that it is a serious problem.

Extract Three

You hear two friends talking about recent changes they have made to their lifestyles.

5 When talking about diets, what is the man doing?
   A justifying his own choices
   B expressing his preferences
   C recommending a particular one

6 What does the woman suggest about having a good quality of life?
   A It relies too much on people doing things that harm the environment.
   B People often confuse it with achieving a high standard of living.
   C It will inevitably improve people's life expectancy.

Grammar

Inversion of subject and verb

1 Rewrite these sentences using the phrases given.

1 People in this office are not expected to commute to work every day.
   No longer ....

2 They are building a gas-fired power plant and also putting up some wind turbines.
   Not only ....

3 As soon as they understood the ecological impact of their plans, they reconsidered them.
   No sooner ....

4 We must absolutely not increase our greenhouse gas emissions.
   On no account ....

5 Our ancestors did not know what effect some technological developments would have.
   Little ....

6 This manufacturing process is definitely not carbon neutral!
   In no way ....!

7 He is more down to earth than most other people I have met.
   Seldom ....

8 It is only when we stop burning fossil fuels that we will have a chance of achieving net zero.
   Not until ....

9 I have never been anywhere where they used so much renewable energy.
   Never before ....

10 You must never ever light a fire in this forest.
   Under no circumstances ....

UNIT 7 GREEN LIVING

Writing

Part 1 essay

Sentence adverbs

1 Rewrite these sentences, starting with one of the adverbs from the box. There are two adverbs you do not need to use.

> apparently   unexpectedly   fortunately
> mysteriously   obviously   unsurprisingly

1 It was lucky that none of the houses in the village were flooded last winter.

....

2 People say that soon 90% of all cars will be electric.

....

3 It is clear that we all need to do our part helping the environment.

....

4 Nobody knows why, but some species of bird are increasing in number again.

....

2 Look at the exam task. Which of the opinions expressed in the discussion do you agree with?

☑ Exam task

Your class has had a discussion on what impact individuals can have on helping to solve environmental problems. You have made the notes below.

> **Areas in which individuals can have an impact on the environment:**
> - transport   • food   • clothing

> Some opinions expressed in the discussion:
> 'Planes won't stop flying just because I choose not to fly.'
> 'People should be prepared to pay extra for organic vegetables.'
> 'It's better to hire clothes for special occasions than buy a new outfit.'

Write an essay for your tutor discussing two of the points in your notes. You should **explain in which area you think individuals can make the greatest difference, giving reasons** to support your opinion. You may, if you wish, make use of the opinions expressed in the discussion, but you should use your own words as far as possible.

Write your answer in **220–260** words in an appropriate style.

3 Read the model answer below and answer these questions.

1 Which two notes are referred to?

2 Which opinion is used? Does the writer agree or disagree with this opinion?

3 In which area does the writer think that individuals can make the most difference?

4 What reasons are given to support this view?

5 Find sentence adverbs in the model answer which mean: a *unfortunately*, b *it can be shown to be true*, c *by most people*, d *it is unfortunately true*

It is generally agreed that there is a need to take action to protect our environment. Nevertheless, there is far less agreement when it comes to exactly what type of action, and who should be taking it. While some insist that only action at government level is likely to have any significant impact, there are, arguably, many things that individuals can also do to help.

Firstly, we can, as individuals, consider what we eat. Although organic food is sadly unaffordable for many, there are nonetheless other choices that consumers can make. The mass production of meat and dairy products damages the environment in a variety of ways, and fish species are disappearing from the oceans at an alarming rate. Not only has it become more common for people to cut down on the amount of meat and fish they consume, but adopting a vegetarian or vegan diet has also become less unusual. Such individual decisions can have a wide impact if consumer pressure encourages farmers to grow more vegetables rather than breed cattle and sheep, for example.

Another aspect of our lives to which we can make changes is how we dress ourselves. More and more people buy second-hand clothes, and people are also starting to turn their backs on 'fast fashion', preferring to buy items that they will keep for a long time instead. This behaviour is having some effect on the fashion industry, although it is admittedly limited.

On balance, it is my view that changing the way we eat on an individual basis potentially has more of an effect than changing the clothes we buy.

---

4 Now write your own essay in response to this question. Use the note about transport and at least one of the opinions. Write your answer in 220–260 words in an appropriate style.

UNIT 7 GREEN LIVING   33

8 Learn and earn

Reading and Use of English

Part 8

✓ Exam task

1 You are going to read an article in which four university students from the UK talk about spending a year of their course studying abroad. For questions **1–10**, choose from the students (**A–D**). The students may be chosen more than once.

Which student ...

1 approves of efforts to make having a year abroad more affordable?

2 says the benefits of having a year abroad outweigh the drawbacks?

3 has promoted the idea of having a year abroad to others?

4 takes pride in having resolved a problem?

5 challenges a commonly held attitude?

6 confesses to having neglected their studies at times?

7 was motivated to learn a new skill?

8 embraced the chance to make lasting friendships?

9 dismisses an explanation sometimes offered?

10 acknowledges that an accommodation option may be unavailable?

Studying abroad for a year

Student A

I spent a year studying abroad, and as I'll always tell anyone who's prepared to listen, every student should do that if given the chance. I was in Madrid, attending language classes at university and staying with a Spanish family. They treated me like a member of the family, and I had a great social life, too, with students at the university, so I'd say I had the best of both worlds. It was altogether a great experience, and I've become a far more independent person as a result. I've met a few people who've had the option of studying abroad, but have decided not to because they don't want to graduate a year later than some of their peers. In my view, when exactly you graduate won't make any difference in the long run, so that's hardly a problem, and they should grasp such a fabulous opportunity while they can! Once they've started working and have more responsibilities, they won't necessarily be able to just drop everything and go abroad for a whole year like that.

Student B

During my year abroad in São Paulo, I lived in a university student residence and there were a lot of other foreign students there, too, who I spoke English with, so my Portuguese didn't improve that much. My advice would be to try and stay with a local family instead, though of course that isn't always possible. If I'd done that, I have to say I might have been less easily distracted from getting on with my assignments in the evenings – as it was, there was quite often a more attractive alternative on offer! São Paulo's such a fascinating city, I never even had time to feel homesick, though that can be an issue for some people. One thing I'm very much aware of is that I was incredibly fortunate to be able to have a year abroad in the first place. Not all my peers were in that position, mainly for financial reasons, so it's good that, at my university at least, steps are being taken to remedy that, by making grants available and so on.

Student C

It's often said that spending a year studying in another country helps students to grow up, and I can't say I disagree. In my case, when I was in Berlin for a year abroad, I found the first couple of months quite hard; six of us shared a flat, and two of my flatmates just couldn't seem to get on – it was silly stuff really, like who'd finished all the milk, or whose turn it was to do the washing up. The others turned a blind eye to it, so in the end, I was the one who got them to sit down and talk – and though it took a while, they eventually became quite good friends. Now, I actually look back on that as a bit of an achievement. I also started cooking for the first time ever, which helped me to make ends meet. Being able to create a tasty meal from just a few cheap ingredients has proved useful ever since. And last but not least, my German improved a bit, too!

Student D

Having the opportunity to spend a year at a university abroad is an incredible privilege, I think. I know many people think it's basically an excuse to have a year off, but in fact that's far from the truth. I speak not only from my own experience, but that of many other students, too. It's true that some people do find it hard to get back into a good study routine once they're back home, and they may have other issues, too, but I really think they'll have gained so much while they were away that the experience will, with very few exceptions, have proved worthwhile overall. In my case, in Singapore, I found that some of the people I was studying with were people I had a great deal in common with. That was actually quite a new experience for me, so I made sure I got to know them as well as I could, hoping we could stay in touch once I was home again. That has indeed happened, which is brilliant.

UNIT 8 LEARN AND EARN

Part 3

Vocabulary – Spelling

2 Complete the sentences with a word formed from the word in brackets at the end. In each case, the missing words have a different internal spelling from the existing words.

1 Your exam results are .... good. Well done! (belief)
2 What are your .... on this matter? (think)
3 This invention has many practical .... (apply)
4 The employee's mistake led to a .... amount of damage to one of the company's machines. (horror)
5 She explained her ideas with great .... (clear)
6 He's very well paid, even though he's actually totally .... to do the job! (qualify)
7 It's better to rely on evidence than .... (assume)
8 There's a very sophisticated .... inside this old clock. (mechanic)

✓ Exam task

3 For questions **1–8**, read the text below. Use the word given in capitals at the end of some of the lines to form a word that fits in the gap **in the same line**.

There is an example at the beginning (**0**).

Example: (**0**) ALTERNATIVES

Apprenticeships

In most countries, there are various
(0) .... to choose from after leaving   **ALTERNATE**
school. After all, not everyone wants to go to
university, and there are (1) ....   **NUMBER**
other ways to acquire skills leading to
(2) .... and rewarding work. One of   **PRODUCE**
these may be to do an apprenticeship. Doing
an apprenticeship usually involves being an
employee at the same time as being trained.
So apprentices are paid, but throughout the
period of the apprenticeship, they are acquiring
the skills and knowledge they need for the career it
is their (3) .... to follow in the future.   **INTEND**
Sometimes they must give an (4) ....   **ASSURE**
at the beginning of the apprenticeship that they will
(5) .... to continue to work for their   **TAKE**
employer for a specific period of time after the
(6) .... of the apprenticeship.   **CONCLUDE**
(7) ...., this is an arrangement which   **NATURE**
is more suitable for some people than for others.
The length of each apprenticeship varies according
to the type of work involved and the apprentice's
(8) .... qualifications and experience.   **EXIST**

Grammar
Relative clauses

1 Add commas to these sentences if they are necessary.

1 Mrs Gibbs who used to work in a laboratory is a very good chemistry teacher.
2 The college where I did my training is in a different city.
3 The company which recruited me is planning to hire more staff next year.
4 This university in which I myself studied has a very good reputation.

2 Rewrite the following information using a relative pronoun.

1 I have had three bosses so far. All of them have now retired.
2 The lecturer mentioned a medieval city. I knew almost nothing about it.
3 There were two positions available. Both of them have been filled.
4 The person I was referring to has resigned.

3 💿 Some of the sentences below contain mistakes made by exam candidates. Tick (✓) the correct sentences and correct the ones with mistakes in them.

1 Students which are going to study here should know what the classes are like.
   ....
2 It was Sheila whose presentation impressed me the most.
   ....
3 I got some useful information from my friend Tom works in a factory.
   ....
4 It is not only doing an activity makes you happy – sometimes just relaxing will help you.
   ....
5 The person they eventually appointed was better qualified than I am.
   ....
6 There are some days which you enter a shop you have never been into before.
   ....
7 That is the college I studied at.
   ....
8 A lot of people were made redundant, which affected the local economy.
   ....

UNIT 8 LEARN AND EARN

Listening

Part 2

1 Write brief answers to these questions about working in a coffee shop.

1 What skills do you think are required to do this job?
....
2 What knowledge do you think might be needed?
....
3 How might working in a coffee shop change your daily routine?
....

✓ Exam task

2 🔊 09 You will hear a student called Tomas Lazlo giving a talk to fellow students about his experience of working in a coffee shop. For questions **1–8**, complete the sentences with a word or short phrase.

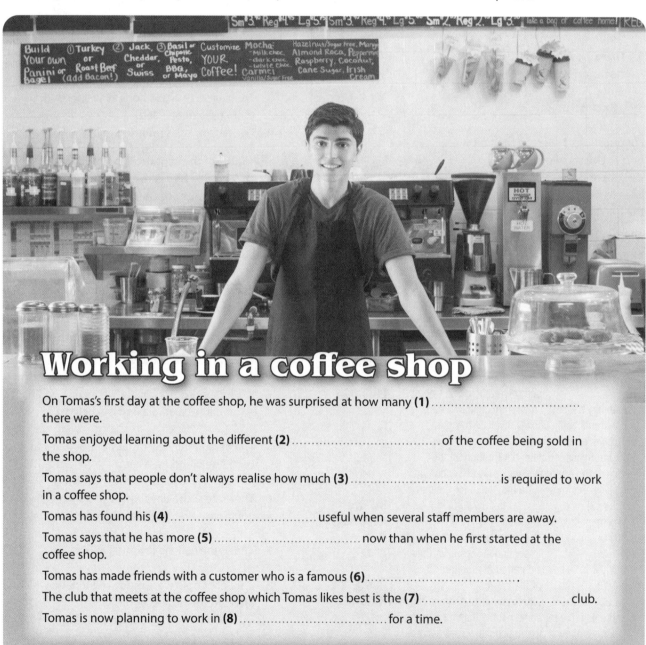

Working in a coffee shop

On Tomas's first day at the coffee shop, he was surprised at how many (1) .... there were.

Tomas enjoyed learning about the different (2) .... of the coffee being sold in the shop.

Tomas says that people don't always realise how much (3) .... is required to work in a coffee shop.

Tomas has found his (4) .... useful when several staff members are away.

Tomas says that he has more (5) .... now than when he first started at the coffee shop.

Tomas has made friends with a customer who is a famous (6) ....

The club that meets at the coffee shop which Tomas likes best is the (7) .... club.

Tomas is now planning to work in (8) .... for a time.

UNIT 8 LEARN AND EARN

Writing

Part 2 formal letter

Formal language

1 Complete each sentence below with a formal phrase from the box.

> find attached my CV   for the position of
> gained valuable experience
> if you would consider   in response to
> should you require   taken every opportunity
> welcome the opportunity

1 I am writing .... the advertisement on your website.
2 I would like to apply .... graphic designer.
3 I have .... from a variety of part-time jobs.
4 I have always .... to improve my English.
5 Please ....
6 I would be grateful .... my application.
7 I would .... to attend an interview to discuss my application further.
8 Please do not hesitate to contact me .... any further information.

2 Read the exam task. What course or courses would you want to do at the English-speaking college? Make some notes on how you would answer the task.

✓ Exam task

You have received a grant to spend six months studying in an English-speaking college abroad. Now you must write a formal letter to the college principal, Dr Perez, thanking her for offering you the place, explaining which course or courses you would like to attend, and telling her how you would benefit from the experience.

Write your **letter**.

3 Read the model answer. Some phrases in the letter are too informal and should be replaced. Underline these phrases and choose suitable alternatives from the box below.

> currently   giving me the opportunity to study at
> I am very much looking forward to coming
> I would be very grateful   improve my analytical skills
> rewarding from a personal point of view

Dear Dr Perez,

Thank you for letting me come to your college for six months. I can't wait to get there in September. I am writing to ask whether it would be possible for me to attend the first-year Economics course, and also the 20th-century English Literature course.

I am keen to attend the Economics course because right now I am doing a Business Studies course, and it would therefore be a good opportunity for me to add to my knowledge in a related area. Studying the subject in English would also develop my language skills and vocabulary in this field, and potentially enhance my employment prospects in the future.

It would be really amazing if I could, in addition, attend the 20th-century English Literature course, because reading is something which brings me great pleasure in my free time and, I believe, provides important insights into the human experience. Not only would learning more about modern English Literature be so cool for me, but attending the classes and doing the assignments would also get me to think about stuff in a more organised way.

Last but not least, whichever courses I attend, spending a significant amount of time in an English-speaking environment will be a fabulous opportunity for me to increase my vocabulary and fine-tune my knowledge of grammar. Your college has a very good reputation for its high standard of teaching and for its lively social programme, both of which promise to provide an enriching experience.

Yours sincerely,

Sara Dupont

✓ Exam task

4 You see this notice on your local tourist office website and decide to apply.

> Opportunities for English speakers to help on tours in the local area this summer.
>
> Flexible hours, all expenses paid, no experience necessary.
>
> Successful applicants will assist tour leaders in a variety of ways, such as helping to entertain children; providing assistance to elderly visitors; giving advice on choosing meals; dealing with unexpected problems and so on.
>
> Write and tell us why you would be suitable for this work and what you hope to gain from the experience.

Write your **letter** in an appropriate style in **220–260** words.

UNIT 8 LEARN AND EARN   37

9 Technically speaking

Reading and Use of English
Part 5

✓ Exam task

1 You are going to read a review of a book about the history of vehicles with wheels. For questions **1–6**, choose the answer (**A**, **B**, **C** or **D**) which you think fits best according to the text.

A Brief History of Motion
James McConnachie reviews Tom Standage's book.

A Brief History of Motion, by Tom Standage, is an exhaustive origins-to-future book, taking in all wheeled vehicles, but focusing on the car. It is full of interesting stories, insights and surprises, such as that British warriors fought the Romans on foot during the Roman occupation of Britain over 1,500 years ago, keeping their horse-drawn chariots standing by as getaway vehicles. Or that 19th-century penny farthings – bikes with a huge front wheel and a tiny back wheel – were only really used in races and displays. Most surprising, though, is the fact that many parts of the world avoided using wheeled vehicles for thousands of years – partly because riding horses was seen as more suitable for people from noble families. What changed everything was a new type of light four-wheel horse-drawn vehicle made in the 15th century in the Hungarian village of Kocs – pronounced 'coach'. It became wildly fashionable among noblemen and soon caught on more widely. That is not the only curious origin of a word that Standage reveals. You might not know that one reason British people stuck with 'car' – which in the past was used to refer to any wheeled vehicle – was that *The Times* newspaper, with its conservative views on language, rejected 'automobile' because it combined 'auto' from Greek with 'mobile' from Latin.

Standage's survey of the early history of the motor car is rapid but entertaining. He has a taste for comic disaster. The first steam-powered road vehicle crashed into a wall on its first test in 1769. During the extraordinary Paris – Rouen race organised by a French newspaper in 1894, seven dogs were run over, one engine's boiler burst, and the driver, Count de Dion, who initially took the lead, got stuck in a potato field. Some things have not changed, although the stories now relate to self-driving vehicles, or autonomous vehicles (AVs), as they are currently known. In the now-legendary 2004 AV race in the US, one AV drove straight into a wall and another 'came to a halt because its vision system was confused by its own shadow'. Later AVs became confused by bikes on racks, a man dressed in a promotional chicken suit and puddles – holes in the road full of rainwater. Ensuring 100% safety proved much harder than getting to 90%.

There are chapters on the Ford Model T, suburban city design and electric vehicles. (Another surprise: the Electrobat electric taxi service thrived in the US as long ago as the 1890s.) A fascinating chapter takes in US teenagers and car culture. In the 1930s, driving out for ice cream and Coca-Cola was referred to as 'coking'. The US focus can be limiting, however. The non-US makes Porsche and Ferrari are mentioned just once, for instance. As for the non-Western world, Standage gives some witty foreign names for shared taxis and reveals, in an endnote, that green traffic lights in Japan can sometimes be blue, because the law there requires them to be coloured 'ao', a word that can refer to both colours. But that is about it.

51 People who are absolutely crazy about cars might find the book slightly **bloodless**. There's nothing on racing. So might environmentalists and health campaigners. Standage hardly mentions particulate emissions from cars, for instance, yet they have been responsible for perhaps 400,000 deaths a year worldwide. But the book is great fun – and was utterly relevant when Standage wrote it. 'We are approaching a fork in the road,' he says. At that time, 'peak car' had indeed already passed and young people were fascinated by smartphones, not speeding around in super-fast cars, and even fewer were even bothering to pass a driving test.

Electric cars, ride sharing and 'micro mobility' (think bike rental and e-scooters) could all be accessed by an app on a phone by the time the book came out. 'In the 20th century, cars granted people independence,' says Standage. 'In the 21st century, the internet of motion promises to grant them independence from their cars.' What we do with that independence is the question. Because as Standage warns, 'what looks like a quick fix today may well end up having far-reaching and unintended consequences tomorrow.' The car transformed the world. This book makes clear that if we want to redesign the future and have a particular vision for how it may look, then we need to act quickly and plan how to best manage the developments we envisage.

UNIT 9 TECHNICALLY SPEAKING

1. What point is implied in the first paragraph?
   A It can be difficult to come up with new names for innovations.
   B The way that innovations are viewed varies all over the world.
   C Important advances can be delayed for relatively trivial reasons.
   D Advances which are not initially thought of as practical may be ignored.

2. What is emphasised about the development of the motor car in the second paragraph?
   A the physical risks humans have taken in pursuit of it
   B the unpredictable shifts in direction it has involved
   C the recurrent nature of a particular aspect of it
   D the lack of concern for safety that has characterised it

3. In the third paragraph, what feeling does the reviewer express?
   A regret that some aspects of the book's subject matter are not adequately covered
   B admiration for the manner in which the writer gathered so much unusual information
   C sympathy for anyone disappointed not to see their own culture reflected in the book
   D appreciation of the writer's efforts to include amusing facts from various parts of the world

4. Why does the reviewer use the word 'bloodless' in line 51?
   A to convey a possible criticism that the book is lacking in passion
   B to indicate that the book may be unlikely to appeal to young people
   C to illustrate how the book has avoided describing anything upsetting
   D to explain why the book has been embraced by experts on road safety

5. In the final paragraph, the reviewer suggests that he
   A has doubts about the wisdom of Standage's approach.
   B shares some of Standage's concerns about what lies ahead.
   C agrees with Standage's view that cars will always be needed.
   D wonders whether Standage's predictions will be proved accurate.

6. From the text as a whole, we are given the impression that the reviewer
   A finds the book immensely engaging despite its shortcomings.
   B applauds the writer for accomplishing what he set out to achieve.
   C acknowledges the difficulties of tackling some controversial topics.
   D considers the book's focus on cars as opposed to other vehicles unfortunate.

Vocabulary

2 Find C1-level words or phrases in the text with these meanings.

a Paragraph 1: complete and including everything
b Paragraph 1: belonging to the highest social group of a society
c Paragraph 2: are about
d Paragraph 4: totally
e Paragraph 5: imagine will happen

Part 2

✓ Exam task

3 For questions **1–8**, read the text below and think of the word that best fits each gap. Use only one word in each gap. There is an example at the beginning (**0**).

Example: (0) OVER

Ada Lovelace

Ada Lovelace, possibly the first computer programmer, was born in England in 1815, well (**0**) .... a century before digital electronic computers were developed. Lovelace drew (**1**) .... many different fields for her innovative work, (**2**) .... languages, music and needlecraft, in addition to mathematical logic. A well-rounded thinker, she created solutions that were well ahead (**3**) .... her time.

Growing up in a privileged aristocratic family, Lovelace was educated by home tutors, as was often (**4**) .... case for girls like her. She received lessons in French and Italian, music and in suitable handicrafts such as embroidery. (**5**) .... common for a girl at that time, she also studied maths.

Lovelace used all of these lessons when she wrote (**6**) .... started as a set of instructions for a mechanical calculator that was being built by the mathematician and inventor Charles Babbage. However, she ended up achieving far more; applying her knowledge of French, music, patterns used for sewing and processes by (**7**) .... cloth was produced in factories, Lovelace is regarded by some (**8**) .... having invented computer programming.

UNIT 9 TECHNICALLY SPEAKING 39

Listening

Part 3

✓ Exam task

1 🔊 10 You will hear an interview in which two scientists, Suranne Curshen and Aziz Khalif, talk about Artificial Intelligence (AI). For questions **1–6**, choose the answer (**A**, **B**, **C** or **D**) which fits best according to what you hear.

1 What struck Suranne about the robots she saw at a science museum?
   A how slow they seemed
   B how few skills they had
   C how valuable they were
   D how amusing they looked

2 How did Aziz get involved in AI research?
   A He met AI experts while doing work experience.
   B He was invited to work on a project at university.
   C He was recommended for a job by a fellow student.
   D He realised he needed to find out more about the subject.

3 How did Suranne feel when she first read an article written by AI?
   A impressed by the content
   B convinced it had been edited
   C privileged to have access to it
   D concerned by the implications

4 Aziz says he doesn't believe AI will replace all lawyers in courts because
   A most citizens would refuse to accept it.
   B the decisions might be challenged too frequently.
   C the preparation for cases is too complex.
   D the arguments made are too sophisticated.

5 When talking about jobs, Suranne believes that in the long-term, AI will result in
   A workers being more productive.
   B more jobs being created.
   C many workers ending up working shorter hours.
   D people having the chance to do more interesting work.

6 They both say that the way in which AI scientists are shown in films may
   A create unrealistic expectations of AI.
   B confuse the public about the role of AI.
   C limit some people's career choices.
   D ultimately lead to inappropriate products.

Grammar

Modal verbs

1 Complete the second sentence so that it has a similar meaning to the first sentence, using the modal in brackets.

1 Barbara took her phone charger with her, but it wasn't necessary.
   (needn't) ....
2 I'm sure I dropped my phone as I was getting off the bus.
   (must) ....
3 It was a bad idea for you to spend so much on a new laptop.
   (shouldn't) ....
4 I think I'll come to the game night, but I'm not sure.
   (may) ....
5 Perhaps my aunt left this camera on our kitchen table.
   (could) ....
6 Surely you don't believe the lies they are spreading online!
   (can't) ....

2 Complete the sentences with a modal verb and the correct form of the word in brackets. Sometimes more than one modal verb is possible.

1 The team got stuck trying to write a new code – I think they .... (use) a different programming language.
2 I don't know why the students didn't understand, because it .... (be) a new concept for them.
3 If this isn't successful, we'll .... (use) an alternative procedure.
4 At first, I thought my phone had too few new features, but I .... (worry) because, in fact, it can do everything I want it to.
5 Their hypothesis .... (definitely be) mistaken, because none of the experiments proved it to be correct.
6 You .... (make) sure that you have taken all the relevant factors into account before you make a deduction.
7 I can't be certain, but I think the methods the scientists used .... (be) flawed.
8 Your theory .... (be) right; it doesn't make any sense to me.

40 UNIT 9 TECHNICALLY SPEAKING

Writing

Part 2 report

Result links

1 Use one word to complete each gap.

1 The timing of the company's work retreat will need to change, ... else only very few people will be able to take part.

2 In view .... the rising cost of living, the platform has had to put up its subscription prices.

3 Technology is advancing all the time, and .... that reason, people are optimistic that a solution to the problem will soon be found.

4 Unfortunately, several applications were not working last week .... account of a system failure.

5 Owing .... technical issues, the number of complaints from subscribers increased considerably last year.

6 There were several reports of minor accidents and .... a consequence, the toy was withdrawn from sale.

2 Read the exam task and the model answer which follows. As you read the report, match these headings with the appropriate sections (A–D). There are two headings that you will not need.

Evaluation of the talks

Ideas for future topics

Recommendations

Introduction

The best talks

Timing

✓ Exam task

Last year, your English teacher arranged for a series of speakers to come and give talks in English about science and technology to your class. Your teacher has now asked you to write a report on this series of talks.

Your report should say what the students thought about the talks, whether or not the times were convenient, and make recommendations for a future series of talks.

Write your **report**.

Talks on science and technology

A ....

The purpose of this report is to provide feedback on the series of science and technology talks arranged for the students last year. Recommendations will also be made for a future series of talks.

B ....

The topics of the talks were carefully chosen to be both relevant and interesting. **(1)** ...., they would not have been so well attended. Many students commented on how fortunate they were to have heard **(2)** .... fascinating speakers. The only talk which proved less of a success was the one on the technology used to genetically modify crops, perhaps because the students were unfamiliar with the topic.

C ....

The talks took place on the first Tuesday of every month from 5–6 p.m. Although the day was convenient for most students, it was felt by many that the time allocated was a little too short. The speakers usually talked for about 50 minutes. **(3)** ...., there was rarely enough time for students to ask more than one or two questions at the end, and the speakers could only give very brief responses.

D ....

Last year's series of talks was **(4)** .... popular that it is very much hoped that another series can be organised for the coming year. Although the day remains suitable for most students, there should be more time after each talk for student questions and further discussion of the topic. One final suggestion is that perhaps the talks could be recorded and made available on the college website for any students unable to attend in person.

3 Complete the model answer with words from the box below. Could you replace any of the result linkers with phrases from Exercise 1?

> consequently   otherwise   so   such

✓ Exam task

4 You recently went on a visit to a science museum with your English class. Now your teacher has asked you to write a report on the trip, giving the students' opinions on the museum, saying what they thought about the practical arrangements for the trip, and making recommendations for future trips related to science and technology.

Write your **report** in **220–260** words in an appropriate style.

UNIT 9 TECHNICALLY SPEAKING 41

10 All in the mind

Reading and Use of English
Part 6

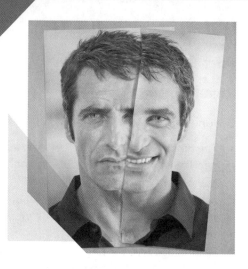

✓ **Exam task**

1 You are going to read four extracts from articles by academics about some research into personality. For questions **1–4**, choose from the academics **A–D**. The academics may be chosen more than once.

A There are many ways of measuring personality, but past research has mostly focused on characteristics that are assumed to be basic parts of our nature. However, new research appears to show that our personalities are not permanently fixed from childhood and that, if we are prepared to put in enough effort, they can become whatever we would prefer them to be. For those of us who have always challenged what are, in my view, exaggerated claims about what does and does not form our personality, these are exciting findings indeed. And although I would not have anticipated them, they do seem to have been obtained using valid scientific methods. This is positive news for anyone who has ever wished they were, for instance, more outgoing, conscientious or optimistic. That we should be capable of bringing about such transformations through our own efforts is surely an idea to be welcomed.

B According to new research, we have the capacity to change our personalities should we so wish and if we are determined enough to do so. I must admit to having been taken by surprise by these findings, because they seem to contradict much of what has been believed about human characteristics to date. Nevertheless, I have no reason to doubt their accuracy. I do, however, feel some concern that if they are widely accepted by policy makers, too much responsibility may consequently be placed on individuals for any problems they are experiencing. The findings must not, I would argue, lead to the conclusion that there is no longer a need to consider the many factors which form our personalities, for better or for worse; in particular, where and who we grow up with, and what we experience as we do so. These factors are crucial, I would argue, in determining what kind of people we eventually become.

C Many people would not expect it to be possible to alter one's personality by sheer force of will. And yet this is exactly what the findings of new research have shown. That this should be an option for us can surely only be to our advantage. The research involved volunteers taking part in regular activities designed to encourage the characteristics they wanted to develop. Very promisingly, the differences in personality that they achieved continued to be evident for several months after the initial training. The results have naturally attracted a great deal of attention, and yet to me, they make complete sense, and could have been foreseen. It is, however, always preferable to have evidence to back up one's hypotheses. A word of caution, nonetheless: no one should imagine that the new findings somehow indicate that young people's surroundings and the communities in which they live have little impact on how their characters develop.

D Recent research suggests that adults' personalities can evolve or even alter significantly, and in particular that people can make this happen for themselves by taking part in some fairly straightforward training. Although these may initially seem to be positive findings, the process may not succeed for everyone. In cases where the hoped-for transformation fails to occur, this may leave individuals feeling even worse than they did beforehand. I was long ago persuaded by the evidence for genetic, as opposed to environmental or any other factors, when it comes to determining personality. I have not seen anything in the new research to make me change my mind. I would even go so far as to question some of the statistics and the evaluation criteria. Moreover, the unexpected nature of these findings leads me to believe that more research is needed before a definitive judgement on their significance can be made.

Which academic

expresses a similar view to B on the influence of social environment on personality?	1
has a different opinion from A about how reliable the results of the research are?	2
shares an opinion with C on whether it is a good thing to be able to change one's personality?	3
has a different view from all the others on how predictable the researchers' conclusions were?	4

Part 4

✓ **Exam task**

2 For questions **1–6**, complete the second sentence so that it has a similar meaning to the first sentence, using the word given. **Do not change the word given.** You must use between three and six words, including the word given. Here is an example (**0**).

Example:

0 My school no longer bans boys from having long hair.
AWAY
My school has ...DONE AWAY WITH THE BAN... on boys having long hair.

1 They advised him not to ignore the value of getting qualifications.
DISMISSING
They advised him .... unimportant.

2 The idea of introducing a low-emission zone has been controversial.
INTRODUCTION
There has been a .... a low-emission zone.

3 The evidence appears to suggest the opposite of the initial hypothesis.
CONTRADICTED
The initial hypothesis seems to have .... the evidence.

4 Nobody was surprised to hear that pollution was increasing in the city centre.
CAME
It .... to anyone that pollution was increasing in the city centre.

5 I'll be sorry if you and your sister have had another big argument.
FALLEN
I hope .... your sister again.

6 Jack gets on well with all his family.
TERMS
Jack .... with all his family.

Vocabulary
Three-part phrasal verbs

1 Complete the three-part phrasal verbs in the sentences below.

1 If you won't listen to me, then I'll never be able to get .... you.
2 I need to read .... the topic before I write my essay about it.
3 When I know the answer, I'll get .... you straight away.
4 My parents keep having to check .... my grandfather because he hasn't been well recently.
5 If people try to push you around, always try to stand .... them.
6 I used to speak a bit of Chinese, but I'll need to brush .... it before I go back there.
7 I don't want to go to the cinema with my cousins tomorrow, but I can't get .... it now.
8 If you come .... any problems with your colleagues, let me know.

Grammar
Wishes and regrets

1 Complete these sentences with the correct form of the verbs in brackets.

1 If only I .... how to fix my bike myself! I'll have to pay a lot if I have it repaired. (know)
2 I wish I .... all those awful things to him yesterday! (not say)
3 If only you .... to my advice! Then you wouldn't be in so much trouble now. (listen)
4 I wish I .... in the countryside, but I have to stay in the city for work. (live)
5 I'd rather you .... me of the situation earlier. (inform)
6 If only my friends .... all their time complaining about their jobs every time we meet up! (not spend)
7 It's high time she .... for a better-paid job. (look)
8 If only I .... to her message! (reply)

UNIT 10 ALL IN THE MIND 43

2 Rewrite the following sentences from Exercise 1 on page 43 using the verb *regret*.

2 ....
5 ....
8 ....

3 Write what you might say or think in these situations, using the words in brackets.

1 You have just made a mess of another easy recipe.
.... (I wish)
2 You don't want your friend to look at your painting because it isn't finished.
.... (I'd rather)
3 You meet someone new and have no idea what to say to them.
.... (If only)
4 There's no more room on your phone for updates.
.... (It's time)
5 Your friend Anna hasn't called you for ages.
.... (I wish)
6 You broke your mother's favourite vase.
.... (if only)

Listening

Part 4

Vocabulary – Adjectives of personality

1 Complete the gaps with words from the box.

| anti-social cool hostile insecure |
| narrow-minded natural thoughtful |
| well-balanced |

1 My grandfather's so .... ! He refuses to accept that people might see the world differently from him!
2 Antonio's rather .... He really lacks confidence.
3 Why is she so .... and aggressive? She seems to want to argue with everybody.
4 Lise's very .... She stays calm and makes good decisions, even in quite difficult situations.
5 My brother's quiet and kind, but also a bit .... He doesn't like going out and mixing with a lot of people.
6 Charlie's so .... He always asks people how they are and helps them if they need it.
7 My friend's fun to be with and knows lots of interesting people – she's very ....
8 Eric's very .... He seems totally happy just to be himself.

✓ Exam task

2 You will hear five short extracts in which people are talking about friendships.

While you listen, you must complete both tasks.

TASK ONE

For questions **1–5**, choose from the list (**A–H**) how each speaker says they met their best friend.

A They were colleagues.
B They shared an interest.
C They had a meal together.
D They both had a similar dilemma.
E They were at a celebration.
F They were members of the same sports club.
G They were seated next to each other.
H They had applied for the same position.

Speaker 1	1
Speaker 2	2
Speaker 3	3
Speaker 4	4
Speaker 5	5

TASK TWO

For questions **6–10**, choose from the list (**A–H**) how each speaker describes their friend.

A knowledgeable about a wide variety of subjects
B modest about significant achievements
C tolerant of difficult people
D unconventional in terms of lifestyle
E trustworthy at all times
F idealistic about humanity
G courageous in challenging situations
H considerate towards others

Speaker 1	6
Speaker 2	7
Speaker 3	8
Speaker 4	9
Speaker 5	10

UNIT 10 ALL IN THE MIND

Writing

Part 1 essay

Concession phrases

1 Complete the second sentence so it means the same as the first. Include the word in brackets in your answer.

1. This is one of my favourite books, but few people I know have read it.
   This is one of my favourite books, ………………………………. (yet)
2. In this auditorium, you'll hear the lecture perfectly from any seat.
   In this auditorium, you'll hear the lecture perfectly, ………………………… sitting. (wherever)
3. You'll have to pay to do the personality test, even if it's very short.
   You'll have to pay to do the personality test, ………………………… is. (matter)
4. Although the presenter wasn't brilliant, we understood her message about personalities.
   The presenter wasn't brilliant, ………………………………. (same)
5. If the children wanted to do something, they were allowed to do it.
   The children ………………………… wanted. (whatever)
6. Paola's very clever, but she found that puzzle quite difficult.
   Paola's very clever. ………………………… (so)
7. That actor is recognised everywhere.
   That actor is recognised ………………………… he goes. (matter)
8. Despite only knowing very few people there, we enjoyed the party.
   We ………………………… we enjoyed the party anyway. (may)

2 Read the exam task. Do you agree with any of the opinions?

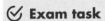 **Exam task**

Careers where personality may matter	Some opinions expressed in the discussion:
• acting • farming • the medical profession	'An actor must be able to play any role, no matter what it is.' 'Extroverts should avoid jobs involving long periods of time alone.' 'Patients value knowledge more than a kind manner.'

Write an essay for your tutor discussing **two** of the careers in your notes. You should **explain in which career you think that personality matters the most, giving reasons** to support your opinion. You may, if you wish, make use of the opinions expressed in the discussion, but you should use your own words as far as possible.

Write your answer in **220–260** words in an appropriate style.

3 Read this model answer. Which careers has the writer chosen? Does the writer have any similar opinions to yours?

In most career areas, it is possible to find many different types of people working effectively. Is it the case, however, that in fact some personalities are more suited to certain jobs than to others?

Take, for example, those working in the field of medicine, such as nurses or doctors. It is vital that these people should be both conscientious and trustworthy. On the other hand, does it matter whether they are outgoing or not? Many patients would probably prefer to be treated by someone calm rather than someone who is too emotional. And yet, it is also important for people in these professions to be considerate and able to express their empathy clearly.

Farming is clearly very different from medicine. Nevertheless, farmers also need to share some of the qualities mentioned above. We need to trust them to produce food that is safe to eat, and no one can succeed as a farmer without working hard. All the same, the attitudes of those who work in farming, along with whether or not they are outgoing or relatively shy and quiet, are unlikely to affect the quality of their work.

It is my opinion, therefore, that in the medical profession, personality has a greater impact on a person's ability to do their work effectively than in a job such as farming. This suggests, consequently, that perhaps those deciding who should study to become nurses or doctors should take candidates' personalities into account at the application stage.

4 Now write your answer to the same exam task in an appropriate style in 220–260 words but …

- discuss acting and one of the other careers;
- make use of at least one of the opinions.

UNIT 10 ALL IN THE MIND

C1 Advanced exam information

Part/Timing	Content	Exam focus
Reading and Use of English 1 hour 30 minutes	**Part 1** A modified cloze containing eight gaps followed by eight four-option multiple-choice items. **Part 2** A modified cloze test containing eight gaps. **Part 3** A text containing eight gaps. Each gap corresponds to a word. The stems of the missing words are given beside the text and must be changed to form the missing word. **Part 4** Six separate items, each with a lead-in sentence and a gapped second sentence to be completed in three to six words, one of which is a given 'key' word. **Part 5** A text followed by six four-option multiple-choice questions. **Part 6** Four short texts, followed by multiple-matching questions. Candidates must read across texts to match a prompt to elements in the texts. **Part 7** A text from which paragraphs have been removed and placed in jumbled order after the text. Candidates must decide from where in the text the paragraphs have been removed. **Part 8** A text or several short texts preceded by multiple-matching questions. Candidates must match a prompt to elements in the text.	Candidates are expected to demonstrate their knowledge of vocabulary and grammar in parts 1–4, and their reading comprehension skills in parts 5–8. Candidates are also expected to show understanding of specific information, text organisation features, tone, attitude, opinion and text structure throughout the exam.
Writing 1 hour 30 minutes	**Part 1** Candidates are required to write an essay, between 220 and 260 words, based on two points given in the input text. They will be asked to explain which of the two points is more important and to give reasons for their opinion. **Part 2** Candidates have a choice of task. The tasks provide candidates with a clear context, topic, purpose and target reader for their writing. The output text types are: • letter/email • proposal • report • review.	Candidates are expected to demonstrate their ability to write at a C1 level. They should be able to demonstrate awareness of style and tone, as well as functions such as describing, evaluating, hypothesising, persuading, expressing opinion, comparing, giving advice, justifying and judging priorities.
Listening Approximately 40 minutes	**Part 1** Three short extracts from exchanges between interacting speakers with two multiple-choice questions on each extract. **Part 2** A monologue lasting approximately three minutes. Candidates are required to complete the sentences with information heard on the recording. **Part 3** A conversation between two or more speakers of approximately four minutes. There are six multiple-choice questions, each with four options. **Part 4** Five short themed monologues, of approximately 30 seconds each. Each multiple-matching task requires selection of the correct options from a list of eight.	Candidates are expected to be able to show understanding of agreement, attitude, course of action, detail, feeling, function, genre, gist, opinion, purpose, situation, specific information, etc.
Speaking 15 minutes per pair 23 minutes per group of three	**Part 1** A short conversation between the interlocutor and each candidate (spoken questions). **Part 2** An individual 'long turn' for each candidate with a response from the second candidate. In turn, the candidates are given three photographs and asked to talk about any two of them. **Part 3** A two-way conversation between the candidates. The candidates are given spoken instructions with written stimuli, which are used in a discussion and a decision-making task. The conversation is divided into a discussion phase (two minutes) and a decision phase (one minute). Candidates are given approximately 15 seconds to initially read the task before starting to speak. **Part 4** A discussion on topics related to the collaborative task (spoken questions).	Candidates are expected to demonstrate competence at organising a large unit of discourse through comparison, description, speculation and expressing opinion. Candidates are also expected to demonstrate an ability to sustain interaction through their use of social language and their ability to exchange ideas, express and justify opinions, agree and disagree, suggest, speculate, evaluate and negotiate.

Acknowledgements

The authors and publishers acknowledge the following sources of copyright material and are grateful for the permissions granted. While every effort has been made, it has not always been possible to identify the sources of all the material used, or to trace all copyright holders. If any omissions are brought to our notice, we will be happy to include the appropriate acknowledgements on reprinting and in the next update to the digital edition, as applicable.

Key: U = Unit

Text

U1: The Conversation for the text adapted from 'Speaking dialects trains the brain in the same way as bilingualism' by Napoleon Katsos, *The Conversation*, 23.05.2016, Copyright © 2016 The Conversation. Reproduced with kind permission; The Conversation for the text adapted from 'How the emoji could help democratise online science dialogue' by Marina Joubert, *The Conversation*, 10.02.2021, Copyright © 2021 The Conversation. Reproduced with kind permission; **U3:** The Conversation for the text adapted from 'Iris Murdoch: what the writer and philosopher can teach us about friendship' by Cathy Mason, *The Conversation*, 09.11.2021, Copyright © 2021 The Conversation. Reproduced with kind permission; **U4:** The Guardian for the text adapted from 'Young entrepreneurs turn their backs on textbooks' by Janet Murray, *The Guardian*, 28.05.2014, Copyright © 2014 Guardian News & Media Limited. Reproduced with permission; The Guardian for the text adapted from 'New year's resolutions: 'I'm going to give away 10% of my income'' by Suzanne Bearne, *The Guardian*, 01.01.2022, Copyright © 2022 Guardian News & Media Limited. Reproduced with permission; **U5:** The Guardian for the text adapted from 'Take more breaks at work, put your head in the freezer … an expert's eight simple tips for better sleep' by Elle Hunt, *The Guardian*, 05.01.2023, Copyright © 2023 Guardian News & Media Limited. Reproduced with permission; **U6:** The Guardian for the text adapted from ''Bake Off for pianos': the spine-tingling talent show that makes people weep with joy' by Michael Hogan, *The Guardian*, 03.02.2023, Copyright © 2023 Guardian News & Media Limited. Reproduced with permission; **U7:** The Guardian for the text adapted from 'The hidden underwater forests that could help tackle the climate crisis' by Lucy Sherriff, *The Guardian*, 02.01.2023, Copyright © 2023 Guardian News & Media Limited. Reproduced with permission; **U9:** The Times for the text adapted from 'A Brief History of Motion by Tom Standage review — when our streets overflowed with horse dung, the car was the solution…' by James McConnachie, *The Times*, 08.08.2021, Copyright © 2021 The Times. Reproduced with permission; The Conversation for the text adapted from 'Ada Lovelace's skills with language, music and needlepoint contributed to her pioneering work in computing' by Corinna Schlombs, *The Conversation*, 12.08.2022, Copyright © 2022 The Conversation. Reproduced with kind permission.

Photos

All the photos are sourced from Getty Images.

U1: ImagesBazaar/Brand X Pictures; Gegham Qalajyan/iStock/Getty Images Plus; **U2:** Feng Wei Photography/Moment; urbazon/E+; Arsty/iStock/Getty Images Plus; **U3:** Halfpoint Images/Moment; **U4:** nd3000/iStock/Getty Images Plus; Edwin Tan/E+; **U5:** Susanne Walstrom/Johner Images; SDI Productions/E+; **U6:** sadrak/iStock Unreleased; Ben Welsh/The Image Bank; Hill Street Studios/DigitalVision; **U7:** paule858/E+; koiguo/Moment; **U8:** Halfpoint Images/Moment; Kingfisher Productions/DigitalVision; **U9:** mikroman6/Moment; API/Gamma-Rapho; Yuichiro Chino/Moment; **U10:** Dimitri Otis/Stone; FG Trade/E+.

Cover photography by 4x6/iStock/Getty Images Plus; Westend61; vladj55/iStock/Getty Images Plus; Sir Francis Canker Photography/Moment; Laurie Noble/DigitalVision; Â©fitopardo/Moment; quintanilla/iStock/Getty Images Plus.

Audio

Audio production by Leon Chambers.

Video

Video editing by QBS.

Typesetting

Typeset by Hyphen S.A.